W9-CYF-869

उद्य
५

richard grossinger

Solar Journal

(oecological sections)

black sparrow press   *los angeles*   *1970*

Copyright © 1970
by Richard Grossinger

Acknowledgment is made to *Monk's Pond, Sou'wester, Stony Brook* and *Io* where some of these sections originally appeared.

SBN: 87685-011-5 (paper)
      87685-012-3 (limited signed cloth)

*As this is my first book, I dedicate it to my teachers,
in their order in my order:*

ABRAHAM FABIAN
MAURICE FRIEND
KINGSLEY ERVIN
CHARLES STEIN
LEO MARX
ROBERT KELLY
DONALD PITKIN
ROY RAPPAPORT

and to my wife, LINDY

NOTE ON SPELLING: *Oecology* is the etymological spelling of *Ecology*. The *logos* of *oikos* is the *law* of the *house* in the deepest sense: meaning the speech by which the house is known to itself, meaning that the house is subject to the proportions of its rule. It's house rules I'm talking about, just and unjust, or finally JUST. I want to recall to you the house, of which planet is one aspect, language is another, body is another—house in the sense that oeconomy is the management of the house and oikumene is the known, inhabited, LIVED IN world.

The house, as *logos*, as *Oecology*, is *imago mundi*, and the subject matter of poetry.

The oecology I am speaking of is distinctly a matter of language. It is not science or conservation, which are commonly spelled ecology, as is anything which pretends to be outside the house and brings that position to bear. The position is stasis, and, in the transformational world that poetry speaks to, it does not exist.

This book grew out of my notes for an ecology course; in that way the title is apt. And the language takes it from there.

Recently in a job interview the man was giving me a purposely hard academic time. That type of talk which goes on easily when nobody wants to talk about anything. He was toying with me for a definition of mythology and magic, which I proposed to teach in a course. He saw them as fun and games, or something like that, hence expendable in a society or curriculum. My own stance was and is that they are the guts of the whole thing, how we know where we are in body, in history, and as individual structure in the objective time of the planets. Somewhere in the course of the discussion I kept saying: use, use, to which the opposite is death, in the most ultimate stimulus deprivation sense. "Ah," he said. "That's just like the argument in architecture: should the house be beautiful or functional. Architects are always trying to decide that, and it's a very important issue . . ."

To which my answer remains: The house has been built, and we've been living in it all these many years, and we're long past the time of deciding whether it's beautiful or functional. We've got to begin living in it.

Ivaluardjuk, the Eskimo shaman, as quoted by Knud Rasmussen:

"The greatest peril of life lies in the fact that human food consists entirely of souls."

— PRE-FIX —

EARTH-DEAF

AND THRU ALL THESE YEARS of history we have been coming to the whole earth, a giant, a god in our skies, the sky itself. We have been coming to the moon, a land behind the earth, behind the veil. We stand before the the temple of Isis; her flowing gown is a river; she is matter, but she is thought; she is indistinguishable; she is Egypt, moon in the sky. We stare thru Egypt into a body, blue with white clouds, in a space so large it fills our eyes, our ears, our nose, our mouth is full of it, breathing; it is woven with spindles of consciousness, giant of which we are part of which we are whole. And its shape. And that it is. And that we are. Where we are. Shaped as we are. The telescope looking back on us looks back into history, pre-Cambrian moon-stone, lizard-earth, earth of ice ages, French traders in Dahomey and the Black Hills. The astronauts see it all, a hurricane in the Gulf of Mexico, a sunspot, Baja, the Big Horns, that it is one. This is earth is the unending energy of body, of giving body to. This is the spinning of worms, the matrix of coccoons, and though the earth is filled with trees in summer, in sunlight, the earth itself is a coccoon hanging from such a tree, the worm spiralling out from earth, holding it on its germinal tail.

And so, passing near the continental moon, whose life is hidden from us, we look back, and over our shoulders as earth rises, the immediate visible god. And this is what they are made of, the astronauts, streaming over the hull of their ship, their direction. They lie in large bionic egg, parallel to the open ducts of conjunction. They are mayflies. They are brought into this temple and the energy floods their openings, white sun in the windows, earth in their heads. It is too easy, with too little energy, that they speak of the magnificent earthrise, that shining blue jewel inlaid with all known history, not the news of the week in review, but herself, dressed as she is, and in the midst of life, stripped, in passion, "you have to see it to believe it," but they are looking too hard, and there is nothing there. While the whole thing that they are, are inseparable from, comes up into the sky, all of history light, and while they look they do not hear, for they think it is with their own eyes; they think they are seeing the earth, but it is speaking to them, lizard on their shoulders, chattering, answering the question they do not know they have come here to ask, telling them what man has almost, what man has always had to know, telling them where they have come; but they don't listen, they are too busy thinking about what they see, that scenic postcard of the west. They think that what it is: is that with their own eyes they can see the earth and with their own ears hear the rush of static in space. It is all speaking to them, and they cannot hear what the voice is telling them, the answer to their questions, for they think it is their own voice, hence trivial, and they are interested only in the meager mechanical powers that have brought them here and will bring them back. They cannot see that the powers are things too, not just the energy that has placed them there, but something about their position once in that energy. They mistake the whole earth for the sum of its parts, as they remember them in leaving; they confuse the mushroom with the drug it contains, cactus lying in the vegetable kingdom, and unconscious, they its consciousness, limited to activity upon their nervous system. They do not know that once they stand inside the mushroom, before the whole earth, the great blue wet god, that it is inside them even as a rocket has taken them to beyond it, even as they have taken the mushroom inside them they are inside the mushroom, and there is a voice of the mushroom, and a voice of the whole earth. They have nothing to ask because they do not hear what they are asking, because they do not know why they are there, that regardless of the Air Force and the United States and the Journals of Botany and the Anthropology Department, they have placed themselves in the hands of a shaman, and reasons are of no consequence, merely paths, grooves, and he is telling them, he is telling us, to look at what it is, it is a whole earth, a unit, whose parts are inseparable, one chemical, acted upon, a droplet, joined anastomosing rivers, there are no boundaries, no conscious breaks in a circle raised to a spheroid, no broken flows, no part of the earth cut off from the other parts, the clouds, the Arctic ice, the open seas, the sun penetrating the whole geochemical bath, building stalks and temples back up heliotropistically; it is a mirror, and in looking in it, we look into the deeply-wound protein chains, thunderstorms of disturbed and active matter, the sea in the whole time of its making, shining with its chemical life: the Stone, gnosis, the inland sea, ourselves, the same. The moon calls men for this vision, a harmonic, before it there is nothing, then earthrise, a blue ball crawling with clouds, living, air sliding upon sea, the mantle rolling on its own metallic density, cerebellum, layer upon layer the rocket passes thru in rising from its pad, as weather, aurora, night, carrying protoplasm, its deed, and other cellular matter from beneath the sea.

It was never anything else, and it is still Pleistocene, still Egyptian; the gods are all around this earth, and the singing is terrific; it is all one, they keep saying, and have been in the Caucasus, the Himalayas, the Appalachians. And now the truth we can no longer avoid, a picture in our newspapers and magazines, the oldest gods in full dress, sun, moon, earth, the wand, the shell, the moon card drawn, body, the waters are body, crab and worm spinning in salt, spider in damp webs, unbroken from island arc to island arc, micronutrients, smoke, thought, the waters are neurons, city, planet news. And now they have come down the river into the open sea, the great Pacific, specific ocean before them, mare and thalassa, at last a name for sea.

SECTION I
INTRODUCTION TO FOOD AND RITUAL

1

THE NORTHERN FORESTS hold the kernel of wheat; but the rich seeded wind moves *thru* the tree-tops spilling only the pollen of gold. The tribes move to the pulse of the caribou, casting ribs and shoulder-bones for direction, casting the sun for a clue to the position of the earth in a garden; the sun goes behind, and the earth is a cozy valley of rain.

The mantle moves like a greedy conscious creature, curls over each hillock, bends around each kane. Here the egg hatches in the garden, where the yellow flower is a fruit, and the high branches of the tree grow conscious and central in the translation of the sun. The magician's wand cracks on a nut of nickel-iron; the second card is drawn; an Empress sits in her local garden of domestic grains, far to the South of the known world. 132,000 parts per billion of DDT settle in the oyster beds of the Gulf. The shrimp die in 24 hours. The peach leaves turn yellow from lack of zinc. The beans starve for boron. And President Lincoln thought so little of trace medicines, he laughed and said, "Soup made from the shadow of a pigeon's wing." And yet the list of remedies is six: 1- Vegetable sugars; 2- Minerals, metals, and salts; 3- Animal medicines; 4- Secretions of morbid tissues, called nosodes; 5- Secretions of healthy tissues, such as Thyroiodine; 6- Macrocosmos, electromagnetism, sun spots, lightning, positive and negative poles, the pull of planets, etc. For which reason Lincoln was shot in a theatre, and the assassin escaped out thru the play.

The world lies just on the fringes on an interpretation, just on the fringes of a text. Some things are wet and blue and live in the mud; some things are red and dry and bed down in the hot sand. And when the pigs are killed, their souls cut loose to heaven, the gods are fed with red flesh of the pig proper, and the blood is the color of war, of territory and hermetic stones around the city, of armed travellers and thieves. The pigs are dead; their bodies are smoked on the fire; the allies feast. The clock of the belly of the pig is reset. Small pigs dance with the women and children. The men move, armed, thru the jungle. On the fringe of interpretation.

We do not know what happens, though we think that hunger is a part of it, and food distributed thru the social network, the political animal fed with the non-political animal, the pigs fed with rumbin until the garden is sparse: the chromosomes of the potato fed to the chromosomes of the pigs, or the place they have both reached in continuous chemical sunlight.

The stone sleeps, silent and transmuting. Its interchange with the earth is fire.

The metal spurts like grease between the bedded sediments. The young stone sends tongues and branches into the older continent. Sandstone injects itself into shale. Sills are harmonious with the lay of land, but dikes cut across the earth. The water-witch, knowing nothing, searching in the endocrine glands.

The rain-dancers reach to a universe between cloud and beast, where rain on earth exists in the mind of the snake as it never can in man, as man can never bring it to earth without some other electrical interference: the snake dance, the cumulus of poisonous injection.

And now divers chase the water-snake, hooked nets which they hold out into the snake's path like men trying to conjure electricity, and the snake flows electrically into their position; they drain its poison on shipboard into a jar: cure for arthritis, neuralgia, rheumatism, the rumbin planted in another racial memory, planted in ash, the neurons flooded by a stimulant long since forgotten in our lethal emergence from water, chemical springs of memory, of forgetfulness—no, of memory! A lesion is cut, mind flows back, track. Cancer breaks thru the code of nucleic acid, changing it to its own, vibrations cracking the temple walls, viral, virile, virulent. The scapula bone breaks along olden lines, manteia, memory—but Lethe, probability.

The story of scapulimancy is this: the shoulder blade is stripped clean of meat by boiling and wiping; it is dried and a handle of wood is made for it. It is held briefly over hot coals; the heat cracks the bone along isobars of 300° C., and free carbon is released, a precipitate of ash. The scapula is then held in a position of predetermined orientation with the topography. The white bone is a *tabula rasa* of the hunting territory, and the cracks and burnt spots are the directions to be followed in pursuit of game. During times of plenty divination is not used in hunting; the leaders pattern the pursuit into areas of previous kill; the animal's territory is kept in the sharp competitive memory of the tribe. But when the animals are overhunted their numbers dwindle, and those left are like chemically unstable pools; they flow instinctively out of the hunted territories, and hide. They are excellent generators of random numbers; the keen knife of predatory intelligence cuts air. But the scapula has no reference to past hunting grounds, though its orientation, after the fact, is one-to-one. The dark lines are tracks along the snow; a new and more perfect map is born in fire. The carnivore once again picks up the lost migratory trail.

The rain-dancers reach to a universe . . . snake . . . electrical interference . . . the cumulus of poisonous injection.

And Reich built a machine to harness such direct conscious energy, for which he was imprisoned, and his books burned by those who run the factories and distribute the milk from the cows. The natives do not understand commerce as we do, though their management of calories and antibodies is fortuitous. What they know is wound in a conscious ring, and can never be repeated and can never have meaning outside itself. The spirits of the high ground are associated with things red, things hard, things hot, things male: they begin the war; their obsessive trump contacts the fighting spirits just as in the belly of Donne's flea the essence of two bitten lovers is fused. They are no longer men; they are the mythological spirits who have always gone to war. Babe Ruth, Joe Louis, Alexander the Great, Geronimo, Mickey Mantle, Chief Joseph, O. J. Simpson.

So the earth is a conscious body, which Spencer touched faintly upon in his electrical sociology: that each action, no matter how animistic, no matter how acasual, begins, is initiated, has efficient cause in, the mind of the enactor. "Universe is the aggregate of all humans' consciously apprehended and communicated (to self or others) experiences —" R. Buckminster Fuller. Every motion, wind thru trees, blue war-paint on the forehead, taste of pig flesh, is as real, is universal. There is no science that is not an ethnoscience, and oecology is the way we plant our fields, the way we contact those who seem to have put us here.

The spirits of the low ground are associated with things cold, things wet, things soft, sexual, feminine, domestic; they quench war, douse it; their pigs are eels; their ions are [OH]$^-$. War flows to a conclusion, pax, in the dolomite caves of ice.

The rain-dancers are concerned with the true kernels of moisture, not the first cells that mark weather on the skin, but the cells beneath those; beneath mood, and beneath thirst; this is where the wet center of life begins, where consciousness of the bird thrives in a wet neural pool. These are the cells that count and lose count, the cells that raise a secret family in the dust; these are the twenty-six golden chromosomes at the end of the treasure map.

There are as many fish in the water as animals on earth. The world forms a chain with itself; what follows resembles what precedes; what precedes resembles what follows. The rain falls; the mouth foams. Sympathy falls in the distance like thunder and lightning. Heavy things are drawn to the sun, light things into the atmosphere; the roots suck the weight of capillary space, heavy gravitation of the planet releasing perfumes and light. If this sympathy were not broken by poison, the whole world would reduce in an instant to a single point. The snake bites the gopher and digests it in a heavy sleep.

Rotation of a chemical sash. The flood is energy or the flood is blessings. The sun bursts from its core, carrying a message to the perceptual tips of the corona, passes thru this planetary skin in charged seeds, entering at the gate of matter. Even a puddle, even a silver coin begins in the sun: a puddle of nutrition in a tree, a coin of the emperor. The tree is sun, frozen into shape by the crystalline exigencies of the earth. The tree seems to be probabilistic but is not. The branches exist in molten shape on the solar core; the tune is played thru the atmosphere; the tune is played thru the volcanic nodes of the earth, as thru a flute. The tree

[15]

exists in seaweed. The skeleton of man sleeps in the secondary memory of halite crystal, in the secondary memory of quartz thru which the shaman places his call.

The bird places his call on high, and the cat mews. (Every child knows that.) A toxin in the saliva of the tick prevents the moose's blood from coagulating. *Dermacentor albipictus* is so numerous on the moose that the host's nervous system is numbed and the animal dies of anemia while the guests at the cocktail party chatter on, sipping from their drinks. The moose dies; the gravid female lays her eggs; the forest is stripped for mining, and the polluted rivers run like diarrhea across the numbed land.

It is the conjunction of fire and water to make Sun that we are interested in, not that other conjunction which releases steam and leaves a silty deposit on the steam-iron. We are interested in hydrogen, the source of the hydrocarbons and octanes, of the alcohols; we are interested in the benzene rings and the snake ouroboros, the dreams of chemists and the return of matter to matter, the king's crown where the solid is released and the snake bites its own tail of carbon. We are interested in the source of ester, peppermint and banana odors on the sun. They are symptomatic. The patient is an organic ring. The patient sits on a perfect cube of hydrocarbons; the royal doctors feed hormones to the king and queen.

God is food, is pig, is thought of warfare, is toss of spear, blue separate from red, is red, is cold and moist, is petrol, is the stormy petrel, is a great petroleum drill on the plains of Oz, is cold and moist, is sulphuric acid, is the urine of the horse, is motion sizzling one step ahead of the cognitive ether, twined in every snap of the bow, is a face behind a dream, is generative grammar, the yeasts rising in the ovens, is seen from a body of frayed whipped skin because that priest is at a slant to the earth and can feel its invisible rays. A positron going backwards meets itself, is an electron, is destroyed in its mirror image. Each item hides a deeper and more discrete item, the muddy liquid hiding a perfect round dance of atomic rings, and they hiding a planetary system of charged shells. Here is where the universe eluded Newton, where he cast out his more obsessive and discontinuous thoughts, which burned in a physical experiment, sparks crackling, the snake spitting light between the spheres, a faint glow filling gap. And the dance of the benzenes is also back and forth, switching between double and single bonds, the house held up in the interim just as the body is during the oscillation of thought, for there is only an interim. In the gap we live.

Each item that burns, leaving ash, sends out a higher gas as well, and that gas burns purer still. Animals squeeze into the world thru a jam-up at the gate; they live there for a while, positron-zebras and positron-flies. There are ten micronutrients essential to plants: iron, manganese, copper, zinc, boron, sodium, molybdenum, chlorine, vanadium, and cobalt. Animals could not withstand the flush of their own systems without iodine; they could not hold their shape without the chemical pull of the moon. Zebra enters on lunar puppet-strings, prances; this is an oecological dance. It is the lack of molybdenum in the soils of Java and Australia that limits the number of nitrogen fixing microorganisms, hence the agriculture of those regions. Temperature and moisture operate together as a climograph of life. The animals jam up at the gate, buzzing like hornets; the angel gives her body. It is dinner time on earth.

2

During the milk strike the Indiana farmers dump tons of fresh white milk into the earth, surprised and sucking it up, as an ancient ocean, as the sun itself. One farmer in Indiana fills a swimming pool with milk; his two daughters, bikini'd, swim in it, splash for T.V. cameras. There is no secret family here to maintain the farm. The girls will turn sour in unexplored chemical secrets even as the milk clabbers. They know nothing of survival, but they are pumping the market, as the automobile market is pumped by girls with very red lips sucking on men's scrotums while they ride in high-priced cars. They are pumping the market but destroying food. The rain cells are replaced with money cells while only the amazed cat licks this holy water from the earth.

And the sea is filled with foreign vessels dragging up the cod and herring and halibut, a picket fence thru which the fish cannot pass into Gloucester or Somes waters, and the men turn to lobstering at 70¢ a pound, Seavey and Phippen, and the Stanleys, sell them to Buzzy Beal or over at Bass Harbor, and they go from there to the restaurants in Boston and New York, five middle men altogether. The Cranberry Islands also bring their catch in here.

The lobster steams in his own juice and sea-water, but a V is cut in the tail of the female bearing eggs, and she is not harmed, either then or afterwards. The adult male turns red in the pot. Black birds raid the fields; squirrels, driven out of the Appalachians by famine, eat the crops of the border states and pour on thru the forest until they reach the sea. Three River buys up cod at 4½¢ a pound.

The fishermen grumble, but the child sucks his own come. The mother chews the proteins of the after-birth. The farm-boy takes the farm-girl into the chemical secrets of his attic. The strike expands. The National Farmers' Organization fills a corral with pigs, and men standing outside the fencing with rifles pick them off, flesh in throbbing piles,

[17]

other flesh hanging alive on meat-picks, the perceptual eye gunning down the herbiverous stomachs, the blind animals who will never see the grassy sky.

A cow, escaped on the highway, Interstate 94, is poked into a trailer while the cops giggle. The great whale is washed ashore, its death proclaimed on six-dimensional totem poles. The steamships come, and the mission ships to the offcoast islands, the fish migrate, and then the great foreign ships come. The cops giggle; the cow broods, its eyes sullen; the fish flaps useless muscles on the dock, breathing out this planet into which it is suddenly sprung.

The poor sick man is turned away from the hospital. But he does not know the secret masonic name of the church. He returns to the slum, the Oddfellows instead. There are too many people. No. There are too many people wanting the wrong things.

The great clock is, is always, reset.

3

The dream is surrounded by a vast system of rails and trains. The dream is the solution to its own problem, and any two ports of call in three dimensions can lie consecutive on the rail system of the dream. The cities of the dream are emblastulated into each other like eggs. The center of the innermost city contains the throne of the dream but not its source. The source cannot be seen thru the window, though the emperor and his court stare out. Swimming pools generally lie above the indoor space of the dream, and a great rush of hollow green water is heard overhead, as the ionosphere which precedes the breakage of color in the sky. The pipes that feed the pool supply the dream with water; the principle is glandular. The shouts of the swimmers can be heard; can be heard the splashes of their dives and the hollow recourse of their body, the swimming pool. Do not let the fruit machine in the lobby fool you. This is not the Y. They are the prototypal swimmers, the eternal swimmers; they need never be fed or clothed because the pool is their continuity. They are irrelevant to the dream as process, but their static is the closest we can come to where the dream begins.

Three times we try to make the trip by plane. Three times the plane fails to rise high enough, and with breath-taking skill the pilot avoids obstacles and returns us to the airport. The hours go by. We eat lunch in the airport. The cold hours at the end of the year creep in. The restaurant is empty. A single unprepared pilot offers to take us in his tiny plane. We climb slowly to a peak; the airplane lands in the dark on the top of a tower. We climb slowly down to the street. We do not know the name of the city. The rumor is that we are committed to process without revelation. We do not know the name or sex or racial origin of the whore, but we come. There is an element of unbroken narrative to this. That is: the narrative is unbroken. The illusion is that we are walking out of the dream. This has been called the road to Oz, and as the story is told we pick up strange creatures, biota, along the way. Actually the road is an illusion. It has no direction as such; it bends back around the city and into the plaza. We begin again.

A sidewalk leads thru a tunnel. Beyond the tunnel is an obelisk. We pass the obelisk and stand in a yard of white pebbles. It is the parking lot to the stadium. There all the players are enacting, in one afternoon, the history of baseball. The sun flashes strobe-like. The fans swarm from the fuzzy detours of sense into the dream, toward the dream, toward and into history; they carry portable radios; each is tuned into one specific game. The airways mix; there is a leak and the swimming pool drips thru the plaster. The baseball field turns damp and cold; ice forms and a great hood contains the atmosphere, the two hockey teams; they play past midnight; the announcers are drunk. We fall asleep in our seats; the game is still on; we leave in the morning to buy some oranges for juice; the guard at the arena door won't let us back in. But it is warm and we are compelled to seek the origin of the river, and the city itself.

The ship moves. Dream city by the river, brick city on the edge of perception, built on the illusion, on the premise that we are alive. A long narrow beach by the river, goes on. And children are running in and out of the bushes, appearing, disappearing, dropping from trees. We are almost there. This is the coastline of the continent where I was first born. This is the hazy edge of the dream. Egyptian hieroglyphs fill the air, dive onto the ship for bread crumbs. Land is almost out-of-sight. Here the air is dim and moist; here we do not know direction any longer, or whether we shall disappear into the softer glands, and be gone from the city forever. The magi would seem to be here, those who first inhabited the continent. The air is hot with sparks, but nothing will appear though the whole zodiac of stars erects itself in memory of the dream's first response to night. The consequences have become vague; we know too clearly we are dreaming. We have prepared our escape if the going gets rough. We are not prepared to be altered here. We awake surprised that there is still time (if time is the same as this velocity of objects in which we hunt).

The dance with the elephant's head on comes before the fire, before the dream, and the fed dreamers sleep on the slow transforming energy of the earth's foods. Digestion offers static, offers grit; they stumble, but

[19]

they do not know where they are. They gather spontaneously, combatting the perceptual distance of the next hill. A crystal precipitates. It is cold. It disturbs the brain-waves. It is snow. The dreamer is shot thru with electricity. He becomes the medulla and the moon sucks him up in a space-suit. He falls back clutching his body, the earth. The ship leads back upriver. The forms are solid and jerky; daylight swims with unclear figures, and a wind-blown sandwich man holds his boards even more firmly to himself as he grooves on the street. Coyote winks three times, and three times the tree shoots twice as tall again; the tiring black bear keeps coming at it. He does not realize who he is up against. This is neither a dream nor a shaman's account of magic. This is the sheer surface of the earth, broken off and rounded, segmented in the pendulum weight of consciousness. This is the ephemeral spruce forest, planted where a woman's hair might anyway grow.

4

A Letter to *Scientific American* (never published there)

The following remarks pertain to the centerfold advertisement by the Polaroid Corporation in your issue on "Light."

The suggested resemblance between these photomicrographs and modern paintings is hardly an accident or a trivial matter. With different traditions of accuracy perhaps, physics and psychology, as well as painting, poetry, etc., are based on and ethically committed to describing the natural world. Miró, Cézanne, Tanguy, and Picasso are part of the same world as Einstein, Heisenberg, Crick, and Watson, and the fact that their discoveries are approximately contemporary to each other demonstrates both the semi-conscious interpenetration of science and the art and the depths to which recognition is a cognitive process whose breakthroughs are discontinuous and, often, virtually acausal. It has long been a fallacy to speak of different traditions of artistic representation as degrees of stylistic deviation from a photographic reality. But this is foolish. In art, as well as in physics and psychology, meaning is either everywhere or nowhere. It is finally tautological and meaningless to say that abstract painting and poetry are exercises in distortion or conscious anti-realism. As such, they would represent at least as much of a problem as the concept of "altruism" does in ecology and animal behavior. Similarly, and with full appreciation of the beautiful Polaroid dyes, it is a fallacy to consider the photomicrographs "documentations" of anything more than an order of light which surrounds and intrapenetrates us completely, right down to our metabolism and proprioception; they are abstractions as well. A sensitive artist is aware of the forces and processes of which he is made; his truth is in presenting none other than what he is. His perceptions are not gratuituous or sufficient; they are an essential derivative of his physiological (inclusive of psychological) position. Their meaning is: that without him they could not themselves be. The scientist has traditionally preferred a world that is here whether or not he views and describes it, but perhaps one of the lessons of modern science is that this view-point often creates more difficulties than it solves.

5

This is the hexagonal lattice, where the homes lie, repeated patterns and subdivisions of which no one man is conscious but in which all men participate as a single organism. The baboons move in the rough perimeter of a nation, certain global trees marking the end of their possible progression. They fall back under a witch's spell; they have drunk the poison; they are born drunk; they fall back into the center. The stars lie outside.

They awake in the morning and seek what is theirs, what lies between the dreaming trees and the edge, what, of its own right, enters their perceptual field. The field is theirs (proprioceptive), and a fight ensues; they destroy what lies beyond their nerve ends with the sharpness of their nerve ends. But the rich fields move like a slow blanket across the dust, first sitting down here, then capturing another plain and submitting it to tangency, fallowness, losing a lee field to the rainless summer and the forty day hot winds.

The conditions for life begin with carbon, the ability of carbon to form rings and long open chains, isomers complex enough to ignite organisms. Psychosomatic diseases begin here; man is a bacterium fed on by viruses. Carbon and its compounds lie beneath this organic chemistry. Moods are chemical; fears and dreams pass like lightning off a hot summer brook. In the streets of the city we see Iodine and Phosphorous, currents of trace elements and trace thoughts, smelly smelling beings passing into and out of each other's perceptual fields. The doctor sits in her office and looks down on the street. It is Dr. Hubbard who offers us these descriptions:

"What does *Fluoric Acid* mean to you? An essential for proper teeth? A question of water supply? A substance which gives an El Greco-ish cast to your skin? A strange light on the avenue? Not so to the homeopath. To him it is Cassanova. A charming, fickle butterfly, the man about town who ogles women in the street, the 'one-night stand' young man with a yen for variety and a great love of strangers . . . .

"If *Sulphur* is the *great unwashed, Magnesia carb.* is the *great unloved,* the illegitimate child, the droopy yet tense orphanage kid, anxious, silent, insecure, with twitching face and fingers and reproachful eyes. With sunken neck and temples, always nibbling for comfort, craving meat, a veritable Oliver Twist . . . .

"Almost anyone with blond daughters recognizes the whimsical, changeable, weepy flirtatious Pulsatilla with their late menses and corpus luteum deficiency, their religious streak in puberty, their jealousy and love of sympathy, their suggestibility, selfishness, self-pity and sanctimoniousness."

This is the chemical environment of earth, the subtle range and variability of carbon rings, the delicate balances of personality and form. All species on earth live between $-200°$ C. and $100°$ C. Land animals can stand a wider variation of temperature than water animals, and, in fact, constant temperature is inhibiting and depressing to most animals. Water is physiologically necessary for protoplasm though 97 to 99% of all water which plants take from the soil transpires thru the leaves. If water and other chemical nutrients are non-limiting in an environment, the energy turned into plants remains nearly proportional to the total amount of energy at the ground surface. The subtle play of temperature, moisture, mineral and metallic elements, gases (such as oxygen, carbon dioxide, nitrogen, and the inert gases), all operating under atmospheric and hydrospheric pressure, all clinging to an uneven topography (shifting soils and lotic stream water) spin out the specific niches into which different animals are drawn, in which different animals make their homes, finally the total community of the earth, seen from outer space as a ball of violent and cyclonic chemical action, brown lava crusts at the base of a chemical storm, oxygen and water vapor in its death.

One of the more barren regions in the terrestrial biosphere is the tundra. Lying between the outermost forests and the innermost rings of perpetual ice, the tundra has reindeer lichens, grasses, sedges, and dwarf willows as its autotrophs. The primary consumers, or herbivores, are reindeer in the Old World and caribou in the equivalent regions of North America. Other tundra herbivores are lemmings and ptarmigans and in the summer some species of insects appear, and there is a temporary abundance of migratory birds. The caribou and reindeer are preyed on by wolves and men. The lemmings and ptarmigans are preyed on by the arctic white fox and the snowy owl.

Most oecological communities are more properly viewed as a web, or a pyramid. The web represents the complex of interlocking food chains, which are never as simple as four classes of organisms. The pyramid, on the other hand, represents the channelling of energy from a great many autotrophs up thru a steadily diminishing number of primary consumers, secondary consumers, etc., to the top of the pyramid, where a small amount of remaining energy is delivered to a correspondingly small number of species, the ultimate consumers who, in turn, are consumed either by microorganisms or by other carnivores whom they may, in fact, also consume.

A marine biosphere consists of phytoplanktonic diatoms and dino-flagellates as the autotrophic level. These include large forests of green and red algae. The primary consumers are copepods, protozoa, mollusks, tiny jellyfish, and some species of minute worms; these are in general known as zooplankton. Among the secondary consumers are those who are attached to the bottom of the ocean or live in sediments of the bottom; this class of ocean animals is called the marine benthos, and includes mole crabs, barnacles, clams, snails, periwinkles, etc. The selective pressure is usually gradual, rarely violent as when one tribe of men chase another from a territory and occupy it. Health and fertility are as important as all pitched battles put together, and the pitched battles between herbivores and carnivores are more important than those between two species of herbivores. The herbivore who can escape the local carnivore best will survive. But if disease should remove his carnivore, he too may be supplanted by another less elusive herbivore with other advantages.

Carnivores make up the classes of secondary, tertiary, and all further macro-consumers. The micro-consumers, or decomposers, break down the delicate and varied compounds of dead protoplasm; these include mainly bacteria and fungi. They turn organic chemistry back into the soil where it can be regenerated in new compounds, both biotic and abiotic, as living plants, or the dead organic material of coals and oils. The life cycle is just one of the many chemical cycles on this planet; in fact, all these cycles participate in one vast chemistry, a chemistry violently altered and punctured by the elements from outside this world that make up the universal chemistry and physics of matter. The planets and stars are all factors in oecological cycles as in meteorological cycles, and the moon alone shapes many of the precise oecological niches of this planet. The stars, who in their own life-spans, consume and re-arrange materials, give off great bursts of radiation which affect chemical life at a microscopic level; the most important of these stars is the sun. In fact, the relation of the chemospheres of the planets to the astrosphere in general may be seen as the relation of microorganisms (decomposers) to the rest of the biosphere. The planets receive the atomic material deadened and consumed as fuel during the star's life; they receive it as the

[23]

one final burst of kinetic energy (nutrition to the earth, as a consumer) that each star gives interatmospherically, vapor rising to the top as great clouds of poison or nutrition depending on which animal you are, the water in constant motion around the lava crusts, water filled with mineral salts and other elements, constantly and violently unto the atmosphere, which itself is electrically charged with the fiery disturbances, from blue to red, of all elements. Yet life exists here: trembling delicate nervous life, life responsive to the full range of chemicals in the storm.

Oecology is concerned with the total set of living and non-living elements in a given portion of the biosphere. The non-living elements are called the habitat, and the living elements make up the oecological community. The non-living elements are the basic inorganic and organic compounds and mixtures of the environment; the living organisms are the biota. The biosphere can be divided in a number of ways, and the first and most significant division is between the autotrophs, or those organisms which nourish themselves, and the heterotrophs, or those organisms which must utilize, rearrange, and decompose other complex organisms. Life could not exist on earth without autotrophs (plants, and most notably salt-water algae), for they convert the earth from a stone on which sun falls into a network in which sun is transformed into vegetation. The autotrophs begin the food chain, and the three classes of heterotrophs feed off them and/or each other. The heterotrophic consumers are divided into macro-consumers and micro-consumers; any community must have both for a complete life-cycle. The primary macro-consumers are herbivores; there are as many species of herbivores as there are species and varieties of plants to maintain them. Two herbivores eating the same vegetation are in competition, though both may co-exist as long as the food supply is ample and the population of either is kept down by carnivores and other demographic factors (such as disease, migration, variable fertility, etc.). If not, one of the herbivores will seize the niche and eliminate the other. The larger and more mobile predators include: the herring-like fish, the cod-like fish, the salmons, the flounder-like fish, the mackerel-like fish, the larger crustacea, turtles, whales, seals, walruses, sea birds, man in his ships, etc. The decomposers are bacteria, similarly distributed to the bacteria on land.

The earth is an ancient and inhabited planet, and man sits on the pyramid of most food-chains, converting the basic oecology of the earth into the manner of relationship in his own sphere, which has become the most important at this stage of the earth's history. Man is an animal, but his cycles and relationships are complex enough to demand the whole framework of the social sciences to describe. Yet the similarity of man to the other animals has long been ignored in these fields. They have emphasized the human components which seem to be beyond the range of any other animal, hence creating a human environment that is "super-organic," an environment into which all men are born, like the organic and inorganic environments, but an environment of symbols and languages and complex man-made objects, an environment which no man can create on his own but which all men, passing on these symbols, participate in maintaining and altering, an environment which would totally disappear with the disappearance of man, leaving no remnants for micro-consumers, except perhaps an electricity in the atmosphere, a complex field most often associated with the magi, able to participate only in matters of the astrosphere.

But aside from all these components of man's actions, there remain oecological consequences in everything he does. Man must consume to survive, and his superorganic environment is first and foremost a highly effective means of competing with certain carnivores with whom man would otherwise be unable to compete at all. Much human activity, no matter what its derivative formations, begins in an oecological field and continues to store vital information regarding exploitation of this field. Man has always stored a vast amount of oecological potential; his systems of classification, no matter how fanciful and acausal, have given the biosphere around him a whimsical and highly-stylized personality. There are so many possible logics and matrices that man eventually chooses a highly effective one. It little matters that the shape of a leaf or the color of a flower has nothing to do with its active medical principle, but there is always something in that active principle that can be coded by shape or color, and this link is reinforced over all other arbitrary ones. Rituals, myths, drawings: serve to recall and reduce the *a priori* arbitrariness of symbols. The science of oecology is, itself, a form of oecological exploitation, itself an arbitrary means of classification.

It might be said that all activities of man have, at the same time, reference to the vast electromagnetic field of the magi (magic), and the vast oecological field of the other organisms. Each action has its intrinsic meaning to those engaged in it, but at the same time, each action establishes the nature of the earth's consciousness, and each action changes the nature of the biosphere and the chemosphere. For instance, most people focus on the higher consciousness in poetry, but poetry, and all human forms of making keep their maker, man, who exists in a highly complex oecological field, perceptually active above and beyond any conceivable exigency of food and health. Man's alertness borders on the ludicrous if compared to the alertness of the other organisms; yet man has passed the point where he has a choice; the opposite of total consciousness is total unconsciousness; if man yielded his forms of making, and reduced his

[25]

activity to *what he saw* as oecologically beneficial, the stimulus deprivation would be enough to destroy the whole human race. At a primitive
level, this relationship can be seen more clearly. Robert Fox gives us a
description of Negrito oecology, and Walter Hough a description of Hopi
oecology.

"The intimate familiarity of the Negrito with nature is the result of a
thorough and sensitive ecological awareness. Many plants have no direct
use or value in themselves, but are important to the Negritos because of
the relationships of the plant with the animal and insect world. The fruits
of some trees are only eaten by birds, but are still very important to the
pygmies, for it is in or near these that bird blinds are built. These particular plants have vernacular names, and meaning to the Negrito, due pri-
marily to this plant-bird association. Specific grasses have local descrip-
tive names only because the pygmies know that they are eaten by the
deer and wild pigs."

"The relation of insects and small mammals to plants in the arid country is very close. Each clump is a veritable menagerie, the insects in the
branches and beetles digging around at the base, and the mice and sper-
mophiles in their burrows under the roots all get shade, protection, and
food from the long-suffering plants, and all are mutually helpful in this
enforced companionship. The Hopi have recognized this relationship
and have assigned certain plants to certain insects or animals which
affiliate, as 'the caterpillar his corn,' 'the mole his corn.'"

SECTION II

DREAMS AND FLESH

1

The mill appears, within distance of the farmer. The smoking factory appears, within distance of the harbor, within distance of the mine. A flower is piped in by its stem. There is an old, a very old language in which this message is spoken. Form assumes where form is. No new material is needed to make new material. It is a code, a hugging, as the grass hugs close to the proteins and mists that feed it, as the eyes and limbs of the baboon bounce and jot along the forest and savanna which keep them turned on. Blake's tiger appears in full armor in the impossibly hot and boring night, excites the pack, attacks the pack, turns off some baboons, eliminates some genes, and moves back along its own close axis, hugging its line of habitation and moving to the central hearth. This is where it all begins, where it is all kept going, where it all is and is because of itself.

The genes and the earth lie in tight coitus; this is a secret society where the totems decide the animals rather than vice versa, as it would seem when men paint their faces and put snakes' heads on. The genes lie like hairs across the surface of another world, a deeper world, the world ruled by kings. This is why even on earth we have royalty, hormonal pecking orders, endogamy, why both kings and subjects expect and assume their roles, rule their natural territories, yield what might be theirs otherwise. Though they are physically terrestrial, they are launched in a land where duchies are a billion years hoary and certain famous crowns have turned from lead to gold. Any signal passed out of this world ends up on earth, earth where the hexagonal lattice rules, where nothing seems to be possible. In fact this other world is the earth, or vice versa, and thru their union, to the ends of each other which are their own ends, they open an impossible and formerly invisible zone of the cosmos: Africa and the Nile, the world ocean, the Indus and Euphrates, fields reclaimed from the sandy outreach of the delta.

Any signal from those shores may be translated into protein and only protein. This is the lost continent, not that it has ever been sunk, but that it has never surfaced, and its surface is filled with shimmering nodes of its mythical possibilities. The level of the earth is genetic, is discrete. What shamans and kings bring with them they can only use in terms of matter and its laws; they themselves can only be protein, and their limitations are protein, though they hold kingdoms in their hands. And messages can only fall between earth and sky. This would seem to limit their content, but it is not the content that draws us or speaks to us, or the content that we can possibly understand or contain. No new material is needed to make what is new. Every corpuscle, whether enormous like

[29]

the brain, or tiny like the redness of the gene itself, contains the *vis* (hence vim or might) of its gate. Thru that gate pass coils so small they are unnecessary to the diachronics of earth science but synchronous to all earth magics. Form finds a form. If it is meant to grow on earth it will find the damp side of a tree, or a tiny marine bloom. The angel babbles continuously; it seems like but is not random variation.

And at night they light the fires, keep warm: sitting in the center, seeking the center. Nothing ceases. Only velocity itself is silent and at rest.

2

We are things across night, and across day. We are dreams, dreamed; we feel our bodies, feel like holdfasts; it won't hold. We are loose; we won't hold. Each flower, face, song is a separate, a new touchstone, Blake's system washed out by saline earth, the Assyrians invading from a higher more northernly order, the wheats extinct, the priests slain, and the costumes of women, the coinage altered, a new race following the glaciers, the Victorian poets, Bill Haley and the Comets, an unknown flower, a flag with strange markings. We awake in the morning and rip the sacrament, the muscles apart; the sunlight pours in thru the nightmare, the old language forgotten, the old words unwritten: not that we speak in tongues but that the very fact of language confuses us: wind thru the trees, trilled "r," the b-s that goes along the park.

The horse breaks reins and leaves the encampment, the rowboat found after the storm at the opposite uninhabited end of the lake, where the lily-pads are thickest and no path leads in from the shore. We are the lights we imagine we see, the saucers, neutrinos, comets, fields of Egypt. We are the planets, our many parts moving separately, a strong fluid passing between cells; we are instantaneous with the zodiac, some parts waxing and other parts waning, some things becoming more possible and other things that were possible dropping below the horizon (though some people still try). We are the disturbance we describe above the Poles, the electricity flaying at our nerve ends, its scars marking our outer garments, and the emblems of nations. We are streaks, glands, diurnal and nocturnal oils, our back arched from horizon to horizon, tingling with birthmarks and the neurons of cities, the fire that pours from our eyes as mammals, as upright yawning stars, now going to sleep. We are the ancient summer lake; the nostalgia we think we feel, as water or honeysuckle, we are, our own water, flooding with images, irrigating our veins with calendrical fruit. We are drunk. We have worms. We are a thousand people wanting to speak, and now one. The sacred language dissolves like limestone, leaving an attractive cave.

"Polly put the kettle on," frog loose in the pond, late afternoon breeze, a chill on the puddle, her hand on the scrotum, rippling the surface waters, the dark waters, as they come across his head. The map leads outward into the green edge of the world, marked with fur and wind-weeds, a world of fire beyond the fuzzy edges, within the fuzzying. The kitten carries a load into morning, sits in the heavy sun, the world torpid and full; there is something inside her, the wet darkness she feels and rolls over on the grass, she will have to open it, go in a dark corner and open it, herself, the tiny bundles falling out, "Polly put the kettle on," cat created in cat by extension of, in properties of code, hidden melody, darkly shaped backbone, squeaking, tumbling into light, the mother cat eating everything that comes out of her except the things crying:

"Wee!
Wee!
It's we!
Here we are."

Wee, who have been born.

The Indians seek their ancestors, those who have been killed fighting the white men; they join together, dancing hysterically, intending to invert the entire earth: the white man gone without even ashes, the fire burning but *restoring* the forest, the flames pulling trees out of the dark-ness, certain children now taking on animal form and returning with the flames, the deer, the rabbit, abundant, the clan abundant, and no one ever again dies. Slowly the sky changes; the Ghost Dance is absorbed into the Earthlodge Cult, many brothers move into white villages; only the single Dreamers persist, and each one has a different ecstatic dream.

Electricity pours into this hemisphere, touching down at shores and in high forests, burning across summer fields and carried in rain clouds, loose voltage in the fish-tank, sealed around the fish, soft closure scar of the fish's eye. The butcher's knife smashes, sets the blood, the electrons loose, lays the pelt in ice, his own heart beating to the rhythm of the knife and block. One bundle is put by another, alike whether they know it or not, red snapper, a dollar ten a pound. Excess parts of the fish collect in another container, heads and tails, the stars that make up the whole body returned to the distal parts of the heavens, gills and fins to separate galaxies, caught in a bleeding pile and plowed into the furrowed farmland, wet microcosm where fire is season, the cat's jellies stirred, poured thru combinations, electricity monthly as even the bubble-glass wheel on the side of the house collects its monthly sparks. Each month we are aged, transformed by what has touched us; each month we pay the electric bill. And when nothing is happening there is no charge, no matter how elaborate our excuse, our artifice, no matter how many showers and creams and nuances of style we use to secure our hold. The price is metabolic, the ovary swelling around the fruit. The moon alone softens all dead bodies, the daylight moon in naps, the moon penetrating dead cells, noxzema jellies, ice, altering bad poems into the archaic language of time.

We sit quietly now. We are tired. We have done nothing all day. We lie in semi-sleep, last game of the season pouring over the cables from New York. No tensions, just this and that, lying in the sun with newspaper and tea. Something begins to happen, something is made of old and rare earths; it is an ancient language. I remember learning it once. I remember that I have always wanted to speak its fluid tongue. We enter a castle, each room is a touchstone; as we enter a room, things change back to what they are, to what they were meant to be.

And though the participants in strobe lights and mixed media claim that the vision must be jarred loose from the outside, we will not respond to being juiced unless we are moving anyway, supplying our own juices, kinetic depth of angels flapping in chaos, wind thru dense branches, yellow patch of marsh herbs, blue colloidal atmosphere, the grape vine, her body's light's heat, flesh of the cloth curtains, blood thru the window, light that sparkles in our sparkling eyes.

And when we went out for dinner on Saturday Mary wore a low-cut dress, lower and lower as she bent and danced around the evening, the slight strains of her body set to an oscillation of revealing, half and gibbous moon popping out of the pie. Lindy at 6 P.M. before we left for their house went thru the closet and found only a giraffey high school dress and wore it unhappily, and Mary at 7:30 doing little spindly dances all over the room, playing with me thru a plastic pillow, a home-built kaleidoscope, loose undesignated energy, nothing could grow here: Lindy is glum and thinks herself unexciting. But, Lindy, don't you see that even though these things always happen and are on T.V. and in movies and tap us out of our lives and would seem to be of importance, we are finally interested only in what we can do and not what irritates us; we are not an oyster making pearls, titillation bounces off previous weariness, rasps, and then we are more sleepy. The dance goes on, the naked dancer, the seductive actress; there is nothing we can do. We will not be pulled in by the light show, in fact cannot be pulled in, except by what we are.

At each moment there is a real possibility, different from the last one; we are arsonists and must light these fires, a small moist blaze in the corner, dark sleepiness unreeling a dream, a spirit awakes, a jinni, and dances, city after city burning in the momentum. And none of this can be provoked, though oysters can be, and the irritant worn by old ladies, their strobe lights in the possession of china and jewels and expensive silvers, trinkets from irritation of an incredible energy, a hydrogen, a sun, but only trinkets, the breasts revealed as the cloth shifts, the bits of perfume in the air. We can use these things, but only as our own. So that, without titillation, the skin is extension of sun, becoming ash, not at once but over years of aging in the corona, a long studied dance, a moist dance, the indirect light of evening, metabolism turning magical powders, old occultisms into what they are, not a Journal of Traditionary Science, but our own bodies, the revelation of our unknown languages, their intersections with the ecologies of earth. There is no holdfast we can apply, river throwing so much mud into our levee that mud itself is what we must grow and harvest, microorganism to whom our body is castle, and innoculation will not drive the holy spirits out or save the body from the river's source. There is a dance to break the boredom; there is a program for Saturday, not on the entertainment page or at a party; the body longs to enter the kingdom and will go anywhere there is energy. But the body, if irritated and toyed with, will settle on another dull, and go back to sleep.

3

The sun strikes the earth's cities like tinder, the bread that was yeast at twilight, now a thin haze in the morning air, having been baked and cooled, the haze rising like an odor from the swamp, from the underground factories, a thousand chimneys leading out crystal to the microcosm, smoke, smoke, the river collecting dust, churning, the sun touching/breeding on the kitchen table, a mold that is food itself, moss on the tree trunk, woman's garments on polished mahogany, she lives here, fishing vessels on lake and rivers, they live here, tropical rains, chemicals of wet and blue light, smoke, water thru stone, jets in the ionosphere, weather satellites photographing, returning signals, face of a gargoyle, ikon of a president carved in the mountainside; the planet is inhabited, and the inhabitants leave their mark. They dig up Lincoln just once more from microorganic time, and rust, to look at his face. Special crews leave for the North Pole to tag penguins and polar bears. A British man sails around the world in a tiny boat. Astronauts orbit above the atmosphere. The earth is a storm, and in that storm live lattices and crystals, live finely-dissected leaves covered with alphabets, stones with petroglyphs, oil wells, irrigated fields, the floating chinampas of Mexico, monumental architecture for sun and moon, tracks of the planets with known paths. Electric current, offshore current, hurricanes mapped as local disturbances, and the houses hold out the chemical rain. Men sail to tropical islands to photograph the eclipse. A trained crew to gather crocodile eggs, to dig up Greek pottery and Acheulian hand-axes. Posses cross the African savanna to collect the seeds of *Welwitschia Mirabilis,* the underground tree, to duplicate its environment in a Chicago museum. It is five P.M.; the early show of stars begins at the Planetarium. This is a planet conscious of its own dimensions, latitudes, history, is a semantic simultaneous planet, the baseball photographed and broadcast the moment it is thrown, strike one!

And who would allow for the inhabitation of Jupiter: that poisonous methane storm, that frozen giant of helium and hydrogen oceans and metallic hydrogen continents, ammonia weather, ammonia winter and ammonia spring. No food, no water, no air, no one can live in chemical hell, everything crushed and lethargic, everything frozen and submerged without context. Jupiter lacks a true archaeology, for no mass conceals a more subtle and more ancient form; Jupiter is a planet of sheer moraine where even the most occult markings are in lieu of consciousness. Subtle tropisms fail to produce a mirror, the face of a woman combing her hair, fail to whirl, to repeat themselves, to know syntax, happen without friction or organic tangency. Jupiter has no genetic code, cannot remember itself, cannot remember its own body, or how large/how far, no proprioception, distal, or proximal, no nerves but violent and alert moves, as a cat moves, seeing sounds and fragments of sounds with her eyes. Its flashing explosions are without history or recall, instantaneous, one and then another. Jovian cycles preserve the essential chaos, the number of explanations never multiplied across the vast geosphere, the number of causes without interior reference. And this is a lie.

We cannot imagine that Jupiter is inhabited.

Yet we imagine the ancient desert cities of Mars, as though Oaxacan or Egyptian, the canals bringing water from the polar icecaps to a dying empire. We can embroider Venus with dense jungles, an age of seeding ferns and lizards, rain forests and quaking bogs. Venus is our mythical past, Mars our mythical future. But what creature breathes ammonia and swims under tons of icy atmosphere; what creature could bear the sight of such a creature without screaming out in panic and dying? On Jupiter the universe is hardly getting down to something interesting; it is getting down to itself, what it is at this distance and pressure, as on earth. But we believe our own melodrama, hence the Garden between fire and ice, between water and stone, between jungle and desert. Jupi-

[34]

ter is a Garden also. Life breaks like a crystal, grows outward, a bud shedding protective hairs, knows itself in sexual feedback; life is methane and ammonia, for methane and ammonia are children of the sun as oxygen and carbon, and are conscious but to other ends. Jupiter is now in the middle of its ammonia and methane history; the planet is mapped, its surface features of grave importance, their geology and weather known; there are many nations on Jupiter, and there are some places considered more healthy and fertile than others. The telescope on Jupiter reveals an historic age, a creature, an emblem of consciousness and commerce as surely as the globe of earth reveals to us our history, Alexander, Genghis Khan, Columbus' route, Cuba as Japan, Captain Cook, the Louisiana Purchase, Seward's Folly, cannibals, Amundsen; the red spot, the bulbous land mass is surely a place of ceremonial and historical significance. To explain it by convection currents and atmospheric pressure is like explaining the forests by an extension of the science of stone. The map of Jupiter, belted in colored latitudinal zones like the forests and tundras and deserts of phytogeography, is an historical puzzle, a map left by unknown ancient sea-kings of another world of which we are dimly and always conscious, a map we cannot deny by reducing it to literal chaotic vectors. Wherever there is matter depth is conscious and violence is history. Jupiter's history is as tragic as our own, as uncertain, as needy of saviors and wise-men, these ammonia-hydrogen life-forms assuming crystalline bodies as flesh but their own flesh, like being conscious only conscious of themselves, accepting as harmonious and optimum the fever and climate of a planet which is their own body.

Hence natural selection is the law by which life exists everywhere in the universe, not just in farm country and on planets with soft evening rains. Inhabitation is a local phenomenon, a tense and rhythmic duplication of local fabric to whatever consciousness is warranted and whatever ends are implied. Inhabitation is like a word game which puns only on the resources it has, hence man a being mostly of water and carbon crystals, but each planet has a special chemistry, a chemistry of one chained element which it calls organic and which moves thru chains to consciousness.

A creature arises on each planet out of the density and richness of material there, out of the froth; this is the true law of natural selection, of microniches; all ends are teleological because all ends are the most eloquent and vital expression of the material being touched. Looking out at the inhabited planet, we must realize that from any particular ring of consciousness, any other, based on different chemical chains, will look like a chemical hell, as earth does from the Jovian observatory on Io. They claim that no one could live in hydrogen, oxygen, and carbon; no one

[35]

could live on such a light world; everyone would float to the sky. Yet the earth is a sign in their astrology, and it has its associations with creatures and events.

Jupiter leaves on Kodachrome a signature of history, of use, of conscious dreaming to undo the enigma. And, as we, the Jovians softly breed, and listen within for the voice of their planet, listen from the North Polar Regions, yes, and in the North North Temperate Belt, listen from the nations of the Equator and the schools of the South Tropical Zone. They are not Esquimaux and Polynesians; they are creatures of ammonia, and breathe ammonia and love ammonia bodies, the curse of flesh albeit, and their dreams are the eternal dreams contained in ammonia crystal and ammonia nerves.

4

The airplane rises with muddy wings. The airplane rises from the April bogs, from the nitrogen roots, rises from the pipes and tunnels of the City, rises like an apartment building, carries all its compartments, all its domestic squabbles and dark festes, quests, carries them *in medias res*, to the South. The airplane moves along the continent, rivers flash by, the coastline unwinds at slower pace, farms, small towns, the edge of a city. I have been on this plane before. I dropped a huge egg thru the bottom of the plane; it smashed atop the capitol shrine, destroying the holiday. Police surrounded the plane when it landed, anxious to catch the defiler. I have been on this plane when it has gone South. I know the touch of engines returning to sand as we land on the Southernmost beach. We must work our way out of the underground by phone calls and messages, by remembering routes dug in the past, tunnels of images, desires feeding into each other, multplying of an internal red color, the central waterway of the dream. This is Florida.

There are girls who have always lived here, woven into complex social fabrics, their bodies spindled like women, spindled just beyond reach. This is the land of baseball card girls, their unforgettable iconic faces wound in blankets; they lie in the bed behind a signature. The signature is something arbitrary; its outer skin is the room number, like 72 or 572, its inner skin is a magazine they hold up to distract themselves, perhaps Redbook, a totally titillating unconcerned goddess; the goddess of ancient winding tunnels and deciduous desiring images, the goddess of sifting powders and perfumes, not one face or two faces, but a sideways look, the goddess of early years, who rules over early years, who rules forever over that kingdom in dreams.

She disappears down long carpeted hallways; she disappears into parties and cocktail glasses and red cars; she disappears into mirrors leaving behind a tangle of phone wires and occult banal messages, obscurely sexual; the connections are heavy on electricity, the electricity is wrapped in velvet; the velvet is wrapped around her breasts, or the angle of her hips, disguising not flesh, but complete in its own sinuous form; they wear bathing suits; they jump on trampolines spreading their perfume like spring; they are attainable only thru the mirrors, only thru the tangled wires they leave behind. They treat me as an object without valence; I am not in their world though they are all around me. There are men in their world, tailored jacks and playboys who spin with them in their tangle, whose clothing only seems to disguise sexual organs; together they are lit illusions; together they do an attractive dance. I said they pass thru me like light.

Their perfume: thru me, like light.

The plane has landed in the deep underground; many of these girls are present but they all have plans. I wish to make contact, to call them, to go thru the process of making dates with them and hope that those dates lead to favors, the unravelling of their ornaments, and something there, akin to their ornaments but made of flesh, beneath. I am surrounded by men who have long ago ceased to live: butlers, bell-hops with messages, maître d's. I am summoned this way and that. So-and-so wants to see me; I knew her so long ago; does she live here? She has a room; we are in it together. I reach to touch her but she tells me I have been wrong all along; she throws herself lazily across the bed, my own lazy fantasy. She gets up and disappears. I try to leave her room but there is only a passage-way thru other rooms. Next door is a girl I have also known once. I enter and she is lying in bed naked, except for sun-glasses. She might be looking at me underneath them. Her boy-friend is in the bathroom shaving. She is waiting for him under the covers, the covers ceasing prior to her breasts. She tells me I can have her in the meantime. I take one step towards her and she laughs; she tells me she was only joking; I take the step back, and then leave the room, and pass thru dark rooms where girls whom I have never seen have their quarters, girls who have come in the darkness of summers to make it with a room-mate, and left in darkness. I go deeper into midnight rooms until they lead out into party rooms, great chandeliers and a woman leading dancing lessons for children. I must get out of this endless lobby onto the beach, out by the ocean. I wait for a phone call. I have been waiting and waiting.

The phone rings, girl calls, but who she is any longer I don't know, I suppose she's the one, or was the one but she says to come down by the wharf. I come out into the sun, great houses marked along the avenue

[37]

by the shore, wharf is an endless boardwalk, leads thru games, arenas, markets, circuses, down underground again thru huge dressing rooms where people are putting on ice-skates, the weather cold and nasty, a hard wind blowing in off the ocean, great waves slicing up to the height of gulls. This the great white ladies do not know, the elderly ice-skaters who lace the rigid skates over their rigid bodies. They do not know where they are being taken; they will never reach the ice, the ocean in storm, the continent washed by tropical rain, by seeds and feathers and wet pebbles; they will be kept dry inside, dry as charcoal and ashes as long as they lace their skates; they are distracted by each other and though none of them have a history they are talking.

The boardwalk is a train, is moving, is moving along the upper beach, moving faster, steam and speed, passing thru stations, passing airports, the boundaries of countries, moving faster than the boards of which it is made up; they scatter and fall thru the woods. I chase from car to car, growing younger and younger, smaller, night falling; I am a child and race thru dressing rooms of elderly men unbuttoning their shirts; I am so fast they do not see me. There is no place to go other than the train itself moving into twilight, and now the morning, everything quiet, the sea rolling in/into the times of history, the glass hotels of our time by the waterfront, and a blonde girl I once knew is dressed in official uniform of the age, she is officially waiting to meet me, and hugs me to that end. My penis grows large against her, spreads, as in times of old she doesn't notice it, or doesn't notice her skin upon which thru clothes the weight presses; she is the woman past and I never had her and if I enter her now, within the eddy of this dream, there will be no return. She spreads her legs, dances contortions as if she wants me on the beach. Everytime I approach her she begins singing a song, drawing an instant audience of which I am part and not just the one; she is a performer, a singer whose sexy gestures are not sex, and were not then; this is child's play. We walk along the beach together hand-in-hand; we don't even ask if we remember old times, each other's; she is a goddess here, and this is her land, and I have entered of my own free will, drawn by the penis, the gland, thru dream.

We do nothing; the day itself grows older, night again, and old women lead silly dances like the cha-cha on the edge of the beach. She is still walking with me, now in her evening dress; it is her kingdom, her clothing changes, she is wearing a large hat with fruit on it, mostly bananas, elaborate to the point of nothing. She wants to stay and watch the dancers, and clap. I figure I should go further along the beach, past the lights into darkness. I am driving a car beneath houses raised on stilts. The stilts hold up porches and there are parties; a girl's long hair hangs down fifty

[38]

feet into the water; I swerve to avoid it! A girl hitch-hiker is waiting by the ocean in a white tennis dress. I pull to the edge of the waves and stop, water crashing in over the car; she gets in and her hand begins to play with me, loosening my folds and making room for blood, as if she knew. She shows me her legs, and leads me up past where she is loosening her dress, the buckles. I roll over in bed into the sea, wake a moment and see what I am as not this, what I am as the roots deep underneath this soft powdery light. I know I am not this, but the gland is flooding, and I want to be had, the girl in her own kingdom, back to sleep where she is, and she is gone.

I drive along a back forest road to pick up a girl. She takes me by the arm, says, "Stop here, let's go for a walk in the woods." We have to ask her counselor for permission first; he says he knows my dream and won't let me. I am trapped in this city and its outlying towns, trapped here by the original plane trip, the temperature of my cock as I was then. I stop to pick up my date from the house on stilts, the wind blowing in off the sea, the party over, everyone made or not made, and ready to start again, or if they are made of light they pass thru each other, never having the other's body from never having their own, and I am the only one of flesh and blood. She is a girl in jodphurs; she says she had it last night and wants it again tonight, as though I had filled out some form by dreaming, requesting that and not her, of which she is the initial and primary form, thru which I will pass. Does she know who I am? I am not of her world. I will no doubt do damage. I am not made of light. She speaks calmly in the non-syllabic, or nonsense-syllabic language of the dream. Is any of this sex?, by name?, and if it happens what will happen to me? I tag along with her, waiting for her to break open and show her favors. It is a dry evening; I want rain, proof the fruit can be busted and is moist inside, continues beyond its allure, rooted at the dream. We drive beneath the great boardwalk train, asleep as boardwalk now, its train lights out, its boardwalk lights on. We drive toward the moon, and as we get further she says, "Take me. Take me!" and all the time within the dream I am trying to tell myself the dream is real. Her mother calls suddenly on the car-radio; she asks what we are doing. I must get out of this city. "Make me now, quickly, while you can," she pleads, and starts taking off her clothes, rubs against me.

No! I must get out of here. It is not sex but fantasy based on denial of my body. I will not be led in. This is Florida, tip of the continent on which I live, tangency against heat and tropics and ocean, but swollen into buildings and alluring clothing and designs, the fantastic over-bloated perfumery ninety miles from revolutions. Politics don't enter in here, only my body which has this bottom where nothing happens; allure is made up of meeting these girls over and over again, these girls I can never have, whom I knew then as part of another world where they still live, a kingdom where they are supported by wealth and subjects, over whom I fantasized and masturbated, preserving an imago at the distance of the marks they left, who have become the nymphs of my dream, these girls whom I have known so long, who were never real, who always trap me by knowing that I want too much, and they have nothing, or can give nothing, woven in the social and physical tapestry they are. Because I have missed sexuality in their world I can always desire it, make a nation out of it, an amphibian in dark waters; I can always be dated by them in dreams, be carried by them as if a physical weight, a person with a name from a family they know, and whose parents know my parents, who can never be touched because I am never there and never was there and they know it.

Florida is the tip of the dream, reached by secret plane ticket, there girls turn young and dance, and everyone I once desired has a room and vivid motions and haunts me in a body made of my desire: that icon, and not their natural flesh, which has aged and wasted beneath the cloths and perfumes. Given form thru my own spirits, they are Trobriand ghosts, dragging my cock thru a night of dream, leaving as a sign/a signet some piece of clothing, as fraternity boys demand in a panty-raid, the fetischist at women's stores, and I in dream, a red car, a pearl or some other piece of the jewelry in their box, a bottle of perfume, the rubbings of soft fabrics in their cunts which are extended of the designs they wear. These are women too without bodies; they have only rooms to back them up, rooms filled with beds and perfumes, the advertisements of their imagined desirability, where they move lightly as the ghost who is in their veins, in veils, having pulled us up like shit thru the pipes and lobbies that run beneath this hotel.

They are children; they have learned their antics from secret communications of their parents', my parents' dreams, have learned that they can be everything by being nothing, who leave their lipstick marks on glasses and tooth-paste ads, who carry a carefully wrapped body, designed, the wraps, by stylized maps, the engraved spores of an underwater plant, visible and breaking out on the surface, the complex of rooms and room numbers, of apartments and local streets and local alleys, they are backed up by a mythos turning neutral signs into sex. They come dancing up the beach to the halfway mark, lead me thru their mother's room, their father's room, to their own room by the same interpolary growth, their own clothing hanging there, back thru the vividness of my own memory, their own signature marking their quarters, and then they touch me, and I stand there almost crying, shaking, saying, "I am only human. This is too large." Roll over like a cat in heat, wanting only to be touched, and they stand there dancing a dance of their external and circulatory muscles, dancing without touch, their names as certain as the names on the envelopes I used to receive from them, their female hand-writing, characters soft on the penis, appearing in the middle distance of a date, arranged somehow but now happening, holding out their bodies for a polite official kiss, withdrawing them and substituting a corpse, and there were grown men, playboys so-called whom I lived next door to in college who had given up real fucking and gone over completely to masturbating like an extinct species of plant going to seed, falling in swamps, bogs, railroad stations, city streets, playmates of the month, and would never lead to anything for lack of flesh and blood and the real door, the race gone extinct for lack of intercourse between man and woman, their seed spilled in subway toilets and on the bed-sheets and they spun grasping.

Yes, the nymphs did live in ancient Greece, and Florida as ancient, classic, rife, lush with inhabited pools, the pool-water breaking onto unknown cunt, their bodies rolled out of saltwater, inhabiting for a second the young teen-ager swimming with her date, the classic lines of the ancient beauty contest, Miss America, each one with lips for a cock, each one a declared virgin posing in sexy undergarment ads and singing, "I want you!," each one blown up into an icon, a nymph by the promoter, all fruit and no seed, nothing to grow, so that my dreams are cast way South, the Graecian, Navaho, Harappan nymphs, remembering from another life what has almost touched my body, the genes like the myth of Bridey Murphy remembering an earlier form, another name and another pattern, fucked or fucking, inward or outward, a girl renting a compartment right next to me on the ancient train South thru Carolina, so that in dream we are living in the same room, and she is calling to me in a hot voice but actually speaking about boys to her friends, opening her arms like rings to hold rain, or for rain to pass thru down. I tumble into dream, the overhead crystal chandelier coming down in the well-dressed body of a girl I once knew, putting her arms around me, undressing me, taking my cock in her hands. I look her in the eyes, there is a code older than this act if it is to happen which we must remember if it is to happen. Now she begins to know. She buries her head in my shoulders and breaks into tears.

5

The moon which is the sand which moves the climates. The moon: seven ducks, a mother and six ducklings, fly in. It is the house of the moon, the round log cabin, the round erogenous zone including at its lips your breasts and your lips, including parts of you in a circle I never knew. Maybe there is something to it that you were born under the moon, your round forehead a phase; this is something I know only in the greatest passion, but there should be some things I know only then. An astrology should be there, not that far from an astronomy; I walk on your moon, lunar body; I am wearing a special suit; it is made of water, it is made of waters controlled by moon rising in me. In this suit I am able to breathe while I walk across your body.

The moon only which is able to deposit in each wave a thousand crabs who must die dried out as the wave retreats. The moon which is inhabited, whose flesh is pocked, the multithousand pores of the creatures who die each pulse.

And the cats who live under the boathouse prowl on the perimeter of the moon. The seven ducks land; the cats move in a single file, a comical column, like cartoon strips, but we see what we have been taught to see, the mother squawking back, the old washerwoman defending her young. So in the same world an artist sits before the ocean in broad daylight, and paints a night-time sea, naked women dancing and strange beings of another lit order in the air. The teen-agers watch him and laugh, the old man's imagination, the chemical film to which rivers lead behind his eyes.

The moon is dead, its body torn apart, the fleshy parts clinging to the stone reef, quivering in silica pockets, the dead skin spread like sand all through the towns. There is sand around the apple trees and sand on the floor of the market. The water which is alive with crabs sifts along the dryness and sinks them in silicon, a dead cellular shore, a planet on which carbon is the matrix of thought, the chemical capable of imposing image upon image. Thought ends where the ocean ends, and the dead skin hardens, and we can see that all the time we lived it was in a fantastic shape as well.

It is an island, an inland along the moon, our own continents inverted on another planet, our inside surfaces forming the outer surface of a globe. This is Long Island, or eLongated Island, the roads becoming sandier and sandier as we move toward the tip. A small town: all the grasses are sedges; all the earth is sand and salt and the leaves of plants keep the necessary moistures within. The ecology changes from within, one family of birds becoming another, and the children carrying pails and shovels out to the beach. On the streets sit the same old artists in their stalls. It is not their time; it is out of time with the moon; it is another moon, an artificial model made by architects and city-planners; the rivers lead nowhere inland, have no pulmonary, natural flow. Their paints are sticky, deposited, the frozen dead shapes we imagine we are, in all our nostalgias coming to this island again after so many years. But I remember orange popsicles and a forest which never grew on the edge of the ocean except when I was there, and where I lived. They have painted a fancy world, realisms, boats, orchards, orchids, sea-scapes, land-scapes, cloud-scapes, faces and towns, a world which doesn't exist and never existed and no one would see it if they were not taught to see it. The thing that amazes me is how blurred everything is if I let it be, how I fall right thru the axis of my perception and there is another planet on this very spot. There are endless connected and discontinuous surfaces, some of them cold, some of them lit and reflecting. I open my eyes for a second under water and see bright green light, a flash which lingers on the cells as a lit window. I feel a dizzyness made partly of the water and my own water as I fall in it. I tell myself, on the edge of the ocean, that I am standing on the suface of a planet which I know only because I have a body. And in telling myself this I have another body, a sash, a counterweight, that answers chemically the necessity of thought. This is the ocean, soft as I am; this is my thought that I am swimming in; this is my painting I make out of the colors I splash, no realism, no sea-scape, but an active canvass of shifting colors and destinations, the combined motions of separate speeds.

The artists sit on their chairs selling pictures, continuing a nostalgic tradition that everyone would like to believe they have, that they would reach to in moments they call happy and sad, happy and/or sad, but they don't know, and it's not the shells certainly but the bodies that secreted the shells and have grown and are others and the shells are washed into the shore:

engravings, markings, the face of the man in the moon, Richard Nixon, accepting his party's nomination, promising a landscape, a hay and saw-dust dream, exact imago paints, not the country as it is which we live in, active chemicals and smokes, but an imagined landscape, unpolluted, nostalgic, free but not because they cannot imagine freedom or what it might be: so like a daydream, a thing which a child makes up, the world he would most ideally have, and finds after making it up that he cannot have, cannot keep dreaming, issuing dream, that it is done and he is not, or it is impenetrable even by the chemicals of his sex, the final pitch of the final game of the final championship, the last of a hundred magical women, and the dreamer lies exhausted, having nothing, blaming it on the dream, and not realizing that the World Series pitcher, the king in the middle of his harem, has even less than he who has dreamed it. (And Merleau-Ponty points out that "Oedipus thinks of himself as a parricide and an incestuous person even though he is so in fact only.") So little weight do we place on the genesis of dreams as

[43]

things in themselves.

Now the swimmer re-enters the ocean, the fish its shell. Now the death-masks of Washington and Jefferson, whose bodies are carried far beyond this present tide, are shown as the republic. The vice-president says he has not had time to write a profound speech, but thought is deep of its own accord; he has not had time to reconstruct a daydream, to promise a kingdom in the same literary tradition as his running mate. This is a daydream we shall never have; the candidate balks at the reality of his selection; the child, having brought the daydreams to ecstatic conclusion, can only begin again and repeat the exact same dream, and those who do not belong to the same literary tradition find this the poetry of irrelevancy.

Nixon: he promises frozen, perfect, ikonic, unmoving, the frontier villages, the imagination of factories at their beginning; there is nothing else to do but live it over again, that someone will write the great American novel and we will all be frozen in it, and our children, and our children's children, Citizen Kane's paperweight, the word rosebud on which not only this film but so many films turn, which is why my wife puts on rosebud perfume, to bring him back by the chemicals of smell, and wears a rose in his lapel. And remember that Faulkner grew less and less conscious as he grew older because he was always trying to say the same thing, weaving a different floral sexual boundary around it, the same thing book after book, until it became too perfect and even he began to lose consciousness of it and know it only as literature, a flood which blisters and breaks for a moment in his book named after Absalom, which has the power to turn the word globular into globy and make iffy out of if, a power which can only be chemical on this planet, and whose active chemicals are morphological and syntactic in poetry, and it is Faulkner and not his character who lives for a moment when the fluids take leave of their source and spill over into language.

It is the edge of the sea, my mother sits/having begun psychiatry in the city; "the waves are emotions, my doctor says," and she sits in emotional calm listening to the sea. But it's not just that they are emotions and we are larger than emotion (sex and we are larger than sex); this is chemically driven, propagated, lambda-nu, the butterflies spun in liquid circles about each other, scorpions claw in claw, tugging sideways, which becomes, at right angles, a dance; this is larger into which we swell, by which we are penetrated at *at least* ten key points of the body, isotasy of toes and neck and breasts, shifting compass points beneath the flesh, shifting seas in directions that once were continents, our emotions yes, but before us, and after us, and wound, bound thru us, and sticking out of us like a piece of torn and still irritated flesh, the sea tugs, chemical we are, and tied in a knot, life is chemical on this planet, takes a chemical form that is, the blonde girls clapping ecstatically for Nixon, the paints issuing from tubes equal to symbols, to passions, emotions to the bad painters on the streets of Westhampton, the compass torn loose by another passion, another magnetic field, and suddenly the gulls in their flight turn east, leaving a *manteia,* a sign, not only in air but on the sand, and in the bones, supplely of which their flying bodies are made, the points of the earth within the earth ground in metal, so that even the currency of a coin changes when the king's crown points down, and into another earth; life is chemical, and emotions are wave-ordered, we feel every change in larger waters, inlets, bays, saline content of the sea and its creatures, water and oil-colors running across our frame and eyes as we pull our heads from sea to air, everything colored as a rainbow, the emotions tied softly to the rhythm of everything, changed by birds and winds and tides and planets so dark and cold we cannot see them or their light, tubes of paints which have no color, but which are color, and space colors; the sea brings in thought, brings in kelp, which is not conscious but which is itself consciousness, made by consciousness, broken off at the binary nodes in the form that consciousness passes even in a computer, or water against stone at the estuary of a river, soft water against salt, and a chemical interzone, a planet as small as certain asteroids, and filled to the brim. This is kelp, each branch splitting on a hard soft anvil, and a thought, or two thoughts, thoughts going both ways, and then both ways again, to form the length of the body, the actual kelp contained in a tiny microscopic space, the initial thought remembered to the ends of planetary space which it can encompass, not conscious but made of consciousness.

So that one artist copies another in the frozen fragments of a remembered perception, life is chemical, colorful, the bloodstream pouring out. Nixon draws a careful picture, but this is not a country which exists or that anyone can rule; it is smaller than life, which nothing is, and Olson and the poets are our politicians, for what their words describe and order we have been and done and cannot help doing again and again. Time is not linear, Stapledon exploding universe after universe, but in a linear consecution, as if God, the Starmaker, were Faulkner, one of those bad Westhampton artists, seeking a masterpiece that will endure, the other secret faces in South Dakota rock outliving the presidents carved there, even in that very space where the same organic rot that changes the era will change them; time is wound in several hot circles, boiling over at several points of time at once. And all the graveyards we pass in Long Island and Canada towns. Dead? No. Simply that they lived at another time and are still alive then.

The artists fade into a picture of themselves selling pictures, huddled on the liquid streets, a mirror of a mirror of a mirror, until there is nothing left, their paints dissolving back into rivers, their speeches into static, and then electrically back into the astrophysical plane, the emotions returning to the waves, buried in anthracite layers beneath the moon, flushed out by rivers and washed back again by shifts in the planet's axis. It is a single conscious mind, a planetary emitting object, permeating with tiny crabs, and each time it touches the image of the shore the thousands are stranded in the dry sun, where there is no perception, where kelp dries into a hard black line of seaweed and garbage, and time stops on an exact photographic image of itself.

6

The parts of the clock turn rusty and the measure fails. The bottle sinks. The mattress is left on the field, the stuffing moist and the coils popping, the juice breeds bugs and mold. The sun does not come up but the whole atmosphere bursting with rain, sleep washing off tin, the tactile edges of the world. We step into this puddle by leaving bed, we awake sopping wet, the Brownian particles of daylight, ceaseless, the water running in the sink, our moist sore eyes.

In the forest the hare moves, her fur wet, her paws muddy and cold. She leaves a haze, a wet ring of colors behind her (an image which Wordsworth pursued in hope of a new day, in hope that the rain and moist colors and changing earth would splash against his imagination and convert its images into gold). The frog shifts his ass from water to land, sits on his blue icy world, his oecology, croaking. The poet writes another line, staving off death. The rain ends, the sun on muddy shallows, the egg hatched in night; Osiris' eye ripped of its scab and poured bloody over the mountains into the world, river of morning, of yeast, bread settling against the coils and turning brown.

The juice settles in his blue eye: the frog leaves his eggs, moves on a vector into the water, the eggs suspended, dropping, developing their own pockets. The fish move; they are not dead fish; they are not alive either. The spoon moves in the bowl; the frog drops his moons, his planets, visceral intestinal, the ships in their orbits; the sailors arising from the morning mud, write on their charts what crosses them; meteors, constellations and watery animals; the fiery wandering sash-weights; they go to their shops in rainy attire, the spume in their eyes, oil slicks on the road, rubber coats and rubber hats and even the policemen in galoshes. A comet hangs in the Chinese sky, the wood-cut over the court of Genji telling him that his court is a-synchronous with the universe, that plagues and famine will hang in the tapestry below the comet, in the lands of the people.

The sky inhabits the earth which gives it color, settling in damp tints of fog and oxide, the rainbow spreading behind the hare crossing Words-worth's eyes as color, the incandescence beginning a poem. The earth is lit like a match, burns in his head, the universe to its edges, dims, goes out, and the earth continues to give off a certain moist light, sometimes called a ghost light, and lives in the mountains and cannot be found by helicopter or Blake's mule, an Indian camp-fire, a pegmatite intrusion in the stony sky. The first hunt occurs in this bubble, Lewis and Clark, the map cut in the head, touched with the signature of the animal kingdom, the bison whose bodies are the body of the planet, the contained blood of Christ, the river of irons flowing ceremonially East. A comet hangs over Idaho, an Indian dance engraved in the stone below, a cinder block covered with mud and worms, and cracks.

"A verbal language, a people without a city, a government without a record, are as fleeting as the deer and wild fowl, the Indian's co-tenants of the forest —" Louis Henry Morgan.

Beth is home is body, is the pose by which the letters come to God asking for their statutes, the real estate page, the planet a hot sash-tow, vacuoles, sailors and cells, vessels afloat on the salty celestial mare, Atlantic, the stars, the letters in sea-water, the differences hidden, occulted by our bodies, occult beginning in the body, occlusion of rays over the horizon by which the sun sets, naming Osiris and the lands of the West, forming a bloody scab for his eye, for his eye to close, for darkness to come thru the stars, *mare noctis* to flood the palaces of the world. The occult enters the morning, the hare occult to Wordsworth, the first animal he sees scampering across the poem, establishing that the day will bear reference to rabbits and creatures in the field, the world sprayed by the equinox of hot dyes, the rainbow rising thru detailed oranges and violets, the eye of the frog blue, the eye of the Hawk, of Osiris. His eye enters the poem and turns it Egyptian; we could be nowhere else this morning, the great Hawk rising above the Rocky Mountains and leaving the mark of Egypt on the aspen trees and on the Roaring Fork River. This is not elusive; this is the way it is if our words invoke a string of worlds and older forests, notched into each other as chemicals, enzymes, the marble quarry turning up Egypt and other chunks of white stone, the salt in the cock of the lover: Hare gives rise to Wordsworth, leaves a haze, Osiris breaks thru the haze, the frog drops his eggs, the planets, on which rise up the sailors to chart the oceans and skies. This is the way of the world, the propelled body whose names are properties and the properties are moving things and histories of things. This is oecology, land of our hunt, the string of meat leading back thru the forest to Diana, and dangling the moon (the Kotex dangling the broken ovary, the string leading out of the womb). We sit in the center of it, shitting, laying our eggs, the shortest route to the moon by digestion, sperm, somnia, not the rocket rising from incomplete metals (clue here is Wynken, Blinken, and Nod for whom the sea was stars and sleep distance). The children lie asleep in the bowels of the ship. The moon, a full goblet, glows on the fishy Mediterranean. The fish, neither alive nor dead, beneath the ship, feed on each other. The radio, radiolaria, touches the shore, a band plays in Greece, bugs moving in the mattress, materias, the lava beneath North America. The ship is our only vehicle, the body, Beth, beginning, birth, carries us from night to morning and back, the shuttle. The light is blue, the eye is blue, the chemicals of blue are red. The moon is yellow, the cookie-dough is yellow; the moon's flower is blue in her hair. Her shit is brown, her cunt is red; the house is yellow, its metabolism reaching the toes with equal lines of heat. Beth is the house; the baby is red; the sky is albumin; baby feeds on sky, the angle of the light is blue. At the horizon the ship is red, Osiris rises bringing the baby into the shore. The radio waves are white, the curve of the earth is yellow; the center of the sun is white. The stations are night and day. The children in the kindergarten are dead, they are dreaming; it would seem from the book of enrollment that they are alive. The hare sleeps and is dead; she lives, and dream is her channel. And all those who have died still live, their continuant in the sun.

The oecology of the earth includes all states, all beings, all materials at all times of life, a complete set of living, dreaming, dying parts, and parts of parts; we do not seek other planets or information about them, even in space probes and science fiction, but a language of our own planet, even if it would seem to be Mars.

7

The wind blows and the ship goes, and the moon blows and the ship goes, gates open and close, seal chemically leaving a blaze of a signature in the sky, massive cellular sky locking the canal behind; the ship goes from inland sea to ocean, from lake to river; the river is ancient, has cut the land to the bone, fills the tub, runs over; its meanders flush the farm-land; its waters settle with the acidic weight of spring. The ship is stranded in an oxbow pond, cut off from the continental trade, the com-merce and drift, the coins and winds between continents and sun-stars; the ship stands in shallow water, its currency is altered and its vowels change, its cargo decomposes, rains down thru zones of climate, warm rain in the epilimnion, soft gases entangling with fish in the thermocline, settling in winter, leaving an occult mark beneath the oxbow surface.

The wind blows and the ship goes, and each generation the ship re-places its body, and each generation the sailors forget the previous seas and move across this one, steering, sea connecting with sea, star to star in the connected sky. They move by code or they move by indirection; they move as the heavens move or they move by calendar; they are total slaves to the moon and other ephemera; they are total slaves to their bodies and the things that move us most.

The wind blows, the water rushes in to fill a pocket of sand, crab into the mud and foam closing the sign above its body; the wind rushes to fill a gap somewhere, to fill a vacuum, to close the circuit, rushes thru North Carolina and Northern Ohio, a draft in the attic, an old man lowers the flag thru the storm; the discrepancy is greater during the tornado season, sun-spots in a fury, electromagnetism and attendant rays rushing to fill a hole; the hole is beneath the earth; the houses are held down by magnets, by the forces between atoms; the houses are crushed by the tornado, women crawling out of the basement with their babies, home-less, a comet sinking the Southern continent; the wind blows, light sand moves over coarse sand, loess settling, marl and sap settling; the ship is blown tumbling thru the air.

The moon blows; the jelly flows; the porridge turns thick in the pot. The mineral waters run thru the town and in the urinary track a yellow stone is left, a gem; the waters splash out of their container, over the banks, and by the force of their falls they are at once turned into tiny white stones, one upon another like eggs. The brain hardens, rain-water hardens; the nodules sink thru lime. A swamp dissolves stones instead of making them; a strong brew loosens the brain, the neurons flow, the elec-tricity conducted along flesh and eyes. In an environment of water all things and remnants of things turn soft and lunar, interchurn.

The moon blows, the dusts flow, the genes separate, wind thru the grasses, the moon diminishes, strands cohering. The body is caught in an inward outward tug of waters, of seasons, of gems; a form propels itself, pulse thru skin, inner waters retaining their cycles, constant to which the moon is tied. The fish who live in fresh waters must pee to keep from popping, the salt in their cells drawing in too much water, the great pumps keeping the ship afloat. The land beneath the sea takes on sunlight in dark layers, neuston wrapped on the surface tension, catching the primary glows and turning them yellow and green, pond-lilies, stalk broken off at the top into bent rippling focal lines, an unknown flower that grows thru the sky, whose roots are in the earth, a lotus above the soft horizon, a sign, incomplete in this world, to mark the sealing of the sky. There is a stone described in Medieval books of minerals; its name is coral, and it is soft when it is in the water but instantly stony when brought into air.

The sign is broken, the lotus is disturbed, lotic water running thru jellies, tearing them into downstream rhythms, spreading oil slick on the city streets; rain and soot stream off the alley window; the stickball game ends, and uptown a pinch-runner is sent in for Mickey Mantle; the fans cheer. On the surface of the water a garden develops, a rich colony of crabs, rotifers, seaweed, worms, the sun gluing them to a single fabric, strand replacing strand, is blown by winds across the surface of the sun; the temperature changes and the creatures in the interior of the sun are released from their pods and float upward thru helium to the corona; there they sing and are nourished. The fish on the bottom of the cold Canadian winter are starved for oxygen if snow collects over ice on the lake surface, sealing their world from the sun; a renegade comet can crash the flask and release all the precious gases, life dwindling; the solution unstable. The temperature changes, the fish sink, and other creatures, signs of atoms and weight, topple thru the sky and settle on the sensitive skin; layer upon layer exchange in the differential temperature of jelly, the penis heated by the specific image of the woman, ikon that could be no other, here in the mud, salt bed, specific salinity, tinge of phosphorous, round eyes, sealing of skin, a mark, an exact chemical mark to which the worm responds, and makes its home, sweats oils, secretion, a protective jelly, a shell, not a symbol but the same thing, the pocking and fertilizing of the earth's skin and the soft skin beneath oceans, the rejoicing and squeezing of grapes under sun.

The wind blows, the temperature changes; the ship sinks to the bottom, its petals falling off; it delivers its bodies, its treasure to the bottom; the body dies, an embryo is left, a capsule of seeds. They collect, spin around each other, feed and nourish *inter alia*; they are separate meri-

[50]

dians; they have different periodicities; they come at different times but to each other's toot. The cars ignite and spurt across the rainy street, the trains in their tunnels, grassland ending at the forest, creatures of the interzone hide, cat and snake shedding the winter; the snowshoe hare puts on the coat of the winter sun; it is the same hare; it is a different hare; it is the same fern that was growing here ten thousand years ago; it is the same diatom, the same buttercup, its cells having divided and formed the same image, the identical ikon raised to sun; it is the same nightingale, thought Keats, and Keats the same man, the same cells as Plato, as Homo Erectus, skin graft from the repeated initial sun.

These things have their own clocks, passing each other in cycles of birth, coming too soon, or too late, swallowed or swallowing, born into a sun, a distortion, of which its blood is made, now pouring in thru the morning curtains, a hot stimulating aether, a wet face in the membranes, the mother sucking up the blood. They are born soft, but shells form around them, long palaces by the occult law of numbers, and kings who inhabit with Pythagorean crowns. The moon-clock spins, items drop thru space, collecting in the city like ambrosia, ragweed, the dust of ancient coal and petrols, pigeon dung on statues, rain, the face cast in bronze, renewed by tradition like the blueberry, the Heath family. Rays and dusts collect on the earth, newspapers in the attic, old unread books, invaded by microorganisms and turning yellow, Greek letters on fraternity flags, fossils, the Platonics, the Neo-Platonics, new top soil, the loose windy leaves of parsnips and carrots, the winds of April, the baseball thrown to open the season, the face in bronze in center field, a baseball card of a dead man, invaded by microorganisms, the new season opened by Marianne Moore, throwing out the first ball and kissed by a rookie catcher, the season opened by the metaphysical poets whose distance is the players on the field and the occult numbers that mark their cities, their batting averages, the ratios of shells and petals, the translator opening a Greek text into the unknown English sun.

This is our history as people, as a people, our genes, each generation of faces, photographic, exact, gargoyles, softly molded by rain, and mold forming after the rain; we are soft; God, we are soft, we are finally soft and cannot change and cannot stop the change and cannot will bone or stone though our implements mimic our faces and our animals are ikonic in the zoos, spores escaping and fertilizing the city swamps with marigold and hepatic, packets of seeds and baseball cards, bingo, Miss Subways; we are all aquatic creatures because our body is made of water; we are all marsh marigold, our many penises dangling; we are creatures made of sun, eating plants, and eating sun, drinking the blood of the golden cattle, the sunny muscles and blended juices, drinking the

[51]

sun out of eggs and baking it in sponge cake, and the namesake of the cake swelling in pores and organs under the sea, drinking the sun out of moths, and the seeds of great bananas, the kingdom, the king engraved in coin, the race in flesh.

Oxygen migrates thru the water like clouds, great cumulus bubbles, cirrus streaks where fish streak; there are trees in this world of ocean, or things named after flowers and trees, animals that are called "the sea anemone" and "the sea pansy," having lymph instead of chlorophyll, they mark the mountainside; they are sessile, immobile; other animals take shade in them. Life succeeds life: stonefly nymphs and mayfly nymphs and the spinning caddis with its nets, thrush follows cardinal, meadowlark follows sparrow, and the wireworm follows the bronze tiger beetle and the burrowing spider. A bare field is covered with crabgrass, then horseweed, then aster, broomsedge, shrubs, pine, oak, and hickory; wren, chickadee, and the nuthatch pursue their trees, and parasites and lizards and field-mice follow; and a jungle is made, a single body of intertwined creatures, tank flowers filling with water, hanging from vines around branches, fish and crabs living in the flowers, bloodless stems sucking the roots of the tree, and larvae left in the basal bark. The wind blows and the sun swirls to fill a pocket, the clayland swelling with form, Betsy beetles dying out and the cranefly larvae taking flight; only woodsnails live now by the sandy shore, and people in the cottage beyond.

The names are important; the names are like fire, the animals created in a blend of perception and form, the ikon of occult numbers sealing on a shape, a system like Blake's angel, a niche where this animal can live. Each small area of land has its requirements; the salty inlet breeds a mangrove colony, or a mangled grove, and sea barnacles come in to make their homes around the mangled prop roots. Each thing lives in its castle, *oikos,* the house of oecology, of pentacles, the castle of the king, each blue or yellow card foretelling a dance, a possible future, each card drawn from the deck, whether swords or hearts, or the stick and drill of the Mayan calendar cogs, is a home, an environment, a holy place where some creature, hawk or tiger beetle, can live; tiny voles under the Arctic ice, seven girls dancing in a circle with the sprigs of spring, a warm bloody hole, microorganisms entering the castle of the dead whale, dying at the heat, the speed of their metabolism, the moon card, the jack of weasels, the moth of yucca-lilies, the honey of bees spun thru flower nectars and maps on the sides of orchids and irises, violet nectar-horns, insect and flower imitating each other from different universes of light, the king of corns, the queen of wheats, man and his crops from opposite ends of the same sun, the negative passing thru the positive, or when the boy sits alone in darkness it is the image of the woman undressing, wrapping

[52]

him in her clothes, her functions, dancing toward him step by step, the imago that draws his sperm, but when they lie together on the bed, the same deck of cards, the same card in fact, her hand moving along his body, her hand taking his parts, then he is aroused directly thru the body, she the chemist and the chemicals directly under paw.

There are different decks of cards, some holy, others of cowboys and others in animal cracker boxes, the holy cards of naked women in gas-station toilets, plus combs, plus a glue that will make the penis stay up long enough inside the castle, the Qabbala shorting itself in the female circuits of the male brain, the cards jumbled, the girl firm but the penis confused, searching for imagos, girls dancing, card after card, and psychedelic sound until there is no sound. Alien spores travel in cases thru empty space, engraved on them the haploid or diploid or polyploid number, the occult number of the home star, carrying either of alternate generations, carrying the dormant generation to the cold planet, a gen-eration of flowers set loose from the active surface of the sun, the dande-lion cut by the butcher's knife, the writing, the Atlantic ocean indelible on the scroll, a Greek text carried by a student of Spenser, the plant grows up in a different universe, a different field, the forms of the plant and all its minute flower clusters travel across empty clocks of ice into a new and more ancient universe, in the willow grove each tree the same, each tree the identical ancestor, ego, father of itself, these are clonal decks that go on and on under the Egyptian sun.

Outside Praeter Annex a few dandelions, in the driveway a catalpa tree, pods around its base; at the rear of the driveway begins a small stream of periwinkle, the blue sticky dogbane with green curled leaves and milky juices, one colony from the same ikon, one follicle of fruits having split, and all its eggs hatched, the seven of wands making a home, and all the wands bright with spring, and each wand piercing an open blue sky; the insects stick to the dogbane, its sweet sexual ring, carry its ikon. The blue flowers begin at a log barrier for the cars and lead to a rose tree, the petals having fallen, the fruit begin to swell under a tuft of stamens. Along the fence is forsythia, its petals forming a smooth adhesive goblet; it comes from the same deck as periwinkle; it is colored yellow and its stem is a bush. Bridal wreath sits atop the periwinkle, surrounds the NO PARKING sign; its buds are just beginning, its sign just entering the terrestrial sky. The bees pass from temple to temple, choosing their own wine to drink, their own gods and sticky penises, and no one can account for taste, the men who gather bras and leave their sperm on pocket books, and those who boil and drink sweaty socks and come in the nocturnal grass, or soak bread in the urinals of other men; there is no accounting for specificity, but specificity it is; the ikon emerges from the specific

[53]

dream of a face, a form outside of another form watching or tasting it, a bronze or blue petalled statue, a specific woman lost on Maple Street, or some enchanted evening, or "will the girl in the yellow dress I saw at the Michigan Theatre please meet me on the diag at noon today," the insect following the yellow map to the specific flower, and resting there, in marsh marigold, or bloodroot, waiting there to sip, to consecrate a cult, perhaps genetic but certainly his own cult of the specific goddess, her own unknown genetic cult as she buys a yellow spring dress at Kay Baums, the ants in dogshit, the flies pollinating the stinking halls of skunk cabbage, orchids growing up in highway projects and on interstate roads, their twisted wings resupine to the flight of bugs, soft forms without vision coming up in larvae, crawling thru the mud into the fire, the giant awaking from a thousand years sleep and recognizing the princess he desired before the volcano, before Hiroshima, before he died suddenly in battle, the genetic crown cut into her face, what she cannot escape is his desire, even as she runs into the sea, the fortune-woman dealing another card, this one from between her legs, the cult which has degenerated into strip tease and a bauble smelling of her thrown to the audience, the big men weeping; this is an archetype and can be found in many different sorts of books.

The next card is drawn; it is a place where all of us can live, I mean two of us, I mean all of us from the same body; it is neither blue nor yellow; it is neither microcosm nor macrocosm nor thermocline, but when we are here it is within, and wherever we are it is the time.

8

The children race thru the Museum of Natural History. The teachers pull the reins on the runaway class and point out the various animals in their natural habitats. But it is really an alphabet lesson; the children know nothing of life in this alien world, how the bear lives and breathes, what passes thru the cellular circuits of the wolves at twilight, or how the bees code dances to one another in the air; they are urban children, children occulted within another magic. The exhibits have been set up by the taxidermists, those artists who belong to a secret order of well-known imagist poets, who have reconstructed these scenes as a text-book of romantic language. The images are pure, definitive with bright natural coloring, action-filled, violent interspecific meetings: the terror of Siberian wolves on reindeer, the giraffes preyed on at the water-hole, the bear clawing a fish. The children are meant to learn of oecological violence, Darwinian selection in each habitat; instead they begin speaking a secret language with the animals as phonemes.

The exhibits in the museum have nothing to do with biology. They are the hieroglyphs of a language, the nodal points of a mythical oecology which is really the law of man, man in his house surrounded by his descendants, the theosophical animals who do him homage and penetrate by their shapes his manner of speech. For many centuries now the animals have evolved from men's habits, Mother Goose from a Mother not a goose, Bugs Bunny from a noisy child not a bunny. The bear is a big man. The giraffe is a man with a long neck. Birds are tribes that fly. And fish are races of swimming people, relatives of the mermaids.

Sodomy lies just on the edge of human experience, animals being attractive lovers because they are so stylized and affected, as girls who want to attract put on zebra stripes or birds' eyes. Animals are exciting to people who desire to cohabit with affectation.

In reality, the Museum is filled with slowly-rotting carcasses, animals killed for the purpose of stuffing, their wounds covered by a skillful needle, their glazed eyes opened to a world where they are seen and do not see. They are killed in peaceful activity and dressed up in war garb by the taxidermists. They are killed while seeking their own ends, and are given the false ends of the imagists and story-tellers. What the children recognize is that there is nothing behind the form of the living animal, its characteristic smell, its genetic movements of dance. There is nothing left of the animal except the most trivial and obvious aspect, of which bad poets and bad artists construct whole schools of poetry and painting. It is robbed of its motion, its true microhabitat, i.e., where it was really found when come upon by armed men accusing it of crimes. The animal is gone, and man can make what he wants of the remnants, the alphabetical letter he sees, the evolutionary shape, the caricature surrounded by a stereotyped habitat, the Latin name, and the Latin name of its most frequent associates, a closed system of signs to which living animals must give their bodies because men do not understand or are unwilling to know the essential meaning and use of their language, the unchanging aspects of syntax and grammar, that are taught like a foreign idiom to the students in the urban schools, who speak a different syntax, who move with a different motion. All these teachers and taxidermists would be imagists, overwrought Victorian poets, when language itself began not as semantics but like God in a whirlwind, lightning in the forest setting the trees on fire and driving the animals out, a whole language discovered in the act, the core of making love, sounds linked originally, pertaining at once to the proprioceptive field of the organs coming to a head in ululation, in naming dancing shout. The words never fail us; the words are there, like our functions, to touch with nerve-ends, roll thru muscular change when we need them.

[55]

No separation between language and thought originally; no separation between them ever. Whenever we speak, no matter the ostensible purpose, this is what we are organically trying to say.

9

The unrelenting clatter of trucks, of surface politics, of military tanks and jets: store-keepers threaten, scraping angrily in the bound network of their business, people on the street glare in the rigid soreness of their personalities, loose spitting wires. Now the heavy-coated men drill down thru the shell of the street, stone snapped and broken off against stone, centuries of penetration accelerated in a roar. The thin protective membrane around the sense organs is cracked; multiply impending sounds burst in, threatening the life. The soft tissue of the world is rubbed against the coarse wall of deadened body and thought, moss scraped from its generative stone. We are turned not only on each other, that we love, but on ourselves, that we are. Parts of food and smoky street air, indistinguishable from poisons, sting the open wound of the body, the slow death of its self-realization. The physicians stand ready with their knives only to cut out the source of our growth, to deaden further the body by removing its frightened, shorted circuits, the only lines along which it can come to heal itself, the only syntax which can channel the poisons into the ecology of renewal. We retreat to the protection of our home.

The world is washed away by sleep and begins again, or, since nothing can begin again, it is submerged: the unbearable weight of the world outside the body into that other world, the dark cellular lake where everything melts of its own abstract nature, even steel, even the sound of stone; they are digested there like food, and even food is digested there, simultaneous to its passage along known tracts. Here the cells, somatic and superficial, oscillating between each other as between two separate spells, two separate dreams, become a third thing, a reality neither so staticky and scraping as to wear us away nor so mercurial that it is an illusion, lost and blown with us. This is the possible groove between meaning and nonsense, between pure identity and code, between what is arbitrary and what is conscious, where the body rests as well, between an interminable sleep and interminable rapping shutters. Here is scar tissue drawn tight across the drum; everything remembered is softened and revealed in translucent stain; all that is present is absorbed in the soft thudding explosion of its neutral presence.

Now the day begins again with the song heard earlier on the radio.

At first it is a song about a snake, frozen and dying by the roadside, rescued by a tender woman and taken into her bosom ("Take me in, tender woman; take me in for goodness' sake"). In Aesop's fable it is a hunter rather than a woman who discovers the snake and takes it home with him; he sets it down by the fireside in hope that it still has some life in it. In either version the snake is revived by the heat and then proceeds to "bite the hand that feeds it," according to Aesop. The hunter chops the snake in half before it can kill his son, but in the song the woman is bitten and realizes that she is about to die from the snake's poison. Like the hunter, the woman is astonished by the act of ingratitude; she does not realize the recoil in her act, the consequences bound only in identity, bound in the literal atomic valences of matter and shape (bound also in morphemes, whereby Aesop can *people* his fables with animals). "You knew damn well that I was a snake before you brought me in."

So the frozen snake, the enigma of the male penis attached in recoil to the personality of the man, warmed by her, rescued and revived by her, comes to enter itself, and becomes itself, comes to enter her as in a dream, a separate secret passion of reflexive verbs in which the see-er becomes the seen. Thérèse becomes Isabelle who holds her clitoris in her lips, who brings her passion as a gift in seeking her own unlimited passion, the room becomes the mirror, and we pass directly, are passed, into the painting of another world, and the smaller painting of a mirror within the larger one, reflecting only the drying paint, the bent back substance of which it is made. This is the only possible means of overcoming our social identities and finding our selves, the sequence by which we speak while several neurons away the mirror of the brain slumbers in mute fire.

The snake is revived, or as in Brakhage's films, the penis itself, drugged, or tricked, in reference to its correlate in the natural world. The self is filled with sudden blood and seeks ends so personal that street-corner gossip retains only shreds of their having been, refusing what personal there is in passion to nurture and sustain the trick, the sleeping beauty sleep. We are released as the ice melts, realizing that we are the water it makes, that we come from it and remember it and thought there was nothing else; we are released from the frozen man who surrounds us, our personality; the half-man, the incomplete man, the semi-conscious shield that refuses to dance; but within the metronome we are an obscure tune, repeated in hymns and love-songs, lost forever, from before the time we were born, like Greensleeves; we can never sing this song, but sometimes if we let it, it will sing us.

It is not that it could be this way, that way, or any other way, either for us or the snake. Some say it is a dream and we are still asleep in an original castle; Jung says the castle is consciousness, the woman who tends it: the anima, and the dungeon beneath the castle, which we also remember in fright, is the unconscious mind. Others call it a mad or almost-mad world in which cruelty is the norm (films of starving children followed by films of executions). But it is the great frozen man who surrounds us, his ice-caps, his frozen joints: the father and mother in the head, full brothers and sisters in the neck, first cousins on either shoulder, hunters poised on glacial horns, second cousins at the elbows rowing across the Bering Sea, crossing into the new world thru its frozen caribou skull, third cousins at the wrists, snapping bows with arrows, culling warm clothes out of the eternal frost, chipping their homes out of blocks of that ice, fourth, fifth, and sixth cousins at the joints of the fingers, almost unable to move from rheumatism, almost forgotten at the distal points of lost consciousness, alive on the pampas and in the Orinoco swamps, a new mind acting out fragments of the old mind which has forgotten it, the shellfish tribes wandering at the Southern straits, still pumped with blood, the nails stand for the seventh cousins, those from a previous history, from a land in the ocean, those whose living current is mere relic and design, the secretion of previous thoughts frozen into cuticle and bone. Whether carried by ship or motor, whether brought from the south north or southwards in search of warm rain, our bodies are remnants of snow and midwives on cold winter nights. But in the head, in the core-fire of the brain, is another state of matter, called plasma, that is the opposite of degree zero, of ice; it is the unfrozen unfrozen again; it is the agitated molecules of a gas agitated further thru the reflex of themselves until they are plasma, are hotter than air, an enclosed atmosphere approaching the enactive sun, or thought which glows at the present when it glows, the mirror in the act of reflecting, the one point at which the frozen cruel man is melted, he who eats children and creates the exigencies of inevitable wars and killing, he who was frozen now foaming at the mouth, almost mad in his ecstasy, in the one moment of possible thought. The uncertain state, hotter than gaseous metal and colder than stripped atoms, is thought, dance-shadow mime of itself, fading in shifting patterns of light, renewed by the light which drowns it; the uncertain state is not the sun but thinks as sunlight, the passion of the woman, of the king at his coronation, the white calm daylight of joy boiling like water for tea; only here in the pot is the shadow melted, is the dark dwarf who visits our dreams dispelled, and we awake not to find a black widow in our bed or an intruder in our bedroom, but an empty house ringing with the silence of our own repose, an empty world inhabited only by ourselves and our inventions. The intruder is darker than any mere robber would be; his appearance in our doorway tilts

[58]

space itself down on us, and we huddle in the corner, revealed as ourselves, as the homunculus approaching its identity. The black widow spider carries more in its bite than the transformation from life into death; it holds the key to several innermore rooms in this house; each room it opens is its bite, is another form of itself.

The snake who, moving across dream, carries the impregnating sperm, the unmarried woman who revives him lying below.

As above, so below.

Our world is filled with intruders, the abominable snowman and the flying saucers lying on either periphery of each other; the former is our forgotten unshaped past, the lost consciousness whose temple-lights have gone out and whose temples lie abandoned in the north, is the dark scroll we unwind in ancient dusty books, geomancies and books of the dead; it is what we no longer have except as we revive it, which hulks like a dead shape in the holiest of mountains of the East; it is also the shadow which is the beginning of our race, the river which is neither Indo-European nor Uto-Aztecan; it holds too the deaths of all previous races, the living embodiments of the furthest ringed fingers, those sun-planets of ice, Uranus the gate, Neptune the hallway, and Pluto the chamber at the end, frozen-glass faces in which life is petrified motion, instantaneous speed of ice, hulks of distal planets marching thru the Tibetan mountains, lighting small star-fires in caves, almost invisible under the cold reflecting mirrors that are breaks in the stars.

Whereas the saucers are hot, plasma, anti-dimensional, boiling on the other side of light; they do not lounge in the bottoms of consciousness with the grotesque mis-shapen wolves; they flicker to the degree of furthest thoughts, hazardous melting points at which existence clarifies and justifies itself by being totally unsure.

So sitting in the bath I make bubbles with the top of the shampoo bottle, flipping it over mindlessly, watching the bubbles roll and yaw in the shifting weights of my body. I hold the cap above one bubble and let little drips fall onto it; its resiliency throws them off. It is long-lived for a bubble; it is keeping me in the bath even though I have already been in the bath too long, my fingers growing old and unusable, my skin cold and drafty at the water-line. I should leave and put on warm clothes, but the bubble is a tease at the edge of consciousness, holds the larger and smaller body in the water at the end of a line. Drop after drop: will I see it when it bursts? Then it . . . . not bursts, but has burst, it has happened before I knew; I cannot sit in the bath, sit in my knowing; there is something else which keeps me here, which measures what happens to me each cold instant. It is not possible to be joined to the bubble as weakly as recognition.

[59]

Beyond the bath there is a bubbling cauldron, hot tea on the stove, consciousness achieving its internal taste, not as when it is sipped, but the taste within that, as the glass which, before it reflects, reflects its own substance: the eyes, the tongue. Consciousness is melted, glaciers trickling down into warm inland seas, cutting the fingers off from the wrists, the wrists off from the head; it is all tribal reflex now, all diffusion, inundated from the inland currents of the lunar brain. Consciousness is melting, but all around the ice age moves on, and with it the hard crustaceous body of human tools, knives and pots honed out of the ice age, men ground as the most specialized moraine of great unconscious beasts, the Titans, the glaciers, movers of a previous world whose pressure was sheer pantheistic force, striking the individual lares and hearth-fires, igniting the pantheons and cruel mechanism of torture and unnatural sex before pouring out into their own burning sea. These cities are remnants of ice, these costumes in which the rulers dress, these lotions they apply to aging bodies as to museum portraits, the deep ice age in which they carve their police legions and legislate with fixed frozen law.

Deep in night there are the ships of night, beings at once more conscious and less conscious than ourselves, who on ancient maps are illustrated as great voyaging vessels, off the coast of the continents and almost as large as them, blown by strange faces who were their communicants in a previous history and now are the eight, or sixteen, or sixty-four winds:

are ghost ships, whose conscious form is vapor, whose apparent image is the thought in which they pass, the sailors who guide them as a product of their being each instant, who throw off shield after shield of unconscious skin, of nails and hair as fuel, who have, can have no other direction than this.

10

The leonine girl appears in a crowd of common people. She is lost from the forest. She flashes thru the crowds christmas-shopping, her orange mane flowing. No one notices; we are reminded of the illustrations of Oz, that magic is present in instantaneous form, ready to leap as sexual response, or mythical identification, or nostalgia, and is finally all three burning in tandem landscape, in oscillating sight, this world and that, the girl is Oz, I want to find her, fuck Oz, and the hot winds of Kansas; it is cold winter Michigan; she is a common girl with the optical illusion of a mane, with the optical illusion of passing from the jungle into the crowds of genetically average humans.

But there are lions among us, even as Della Porta's ass stands on the Sears Roebuck corner hee-hawing for Wallace, and the girl, who carries leonine trace, passes among us with her round hat-boxes tied to one axis, a hat to match her mane and orange pants, enters the solar system with a fiery tail, and the astronomers of many nations take attention, charter boats, and move out into the clear atmosphere of the Southern islands to photograph her in naked elemental atoms while she shakes her tail at them. The male lions howl; the comet leaves a gas smelling of cats in heat, female leonine estrus. Magic begins at home, in the lion's den, or better: magic begins at K-Mart and outside Sears Roebuck where the creatures of another world, the animals of a previous creation, mill in human costume. The lion sleeps: an old rock and roll song. The lion dances. The lion leaves no foot-prints in a cloud chamber, silent king of the jungle, bearded hierophant of the chart of elements and elementals: lithium, fluorine, zinc. The lion searches in magical lands for his courage; black panthers move thru the city in Halloween costumes, hold-up men; the speculators with empty cups hoard their gold, thousands and billions of dollars spent on diseases of the elderly, keeping them alive in their apartment overlooking the Renaissance perspective of the park. The lion moves thru the jungle cleaning the bones of the dead and the weak, turning hoarded gold back into genetic rivers. Her ass is shaped in orange fur, fire leading lit into an unknown world Aladdin finds when he dares to rub his cock while looking at her, while the guiding comet moves thru his birth skies, a thin film passing over his eyes, the pure intense orange of vision itself. The African kings move thru the deck of cards, sweeping up royalty, undressing the elaborate jacks, raping the fat queens. The costumes they wore dissolve; they return to an earlier age now that the body lies naked outside the game, and the clitoris, the immediate flesh and not the hard crown, is honored. The comet cleans up the lingering history of the city, the giant wet street-cleaner softening the dirt of a useless history, moving thru the dream with great wet brushes; this is the penis in the lion's mouth, hot breath thru the cunt hairs; this is the body that leaves no foot-prints, the fire which, when properly naked, returns to the sky.

SECTION III
FOODS & POISONS

The sun shines; the birds come down the branches of the tree, step by step onto the sidewalk, wings opening, closing, opening, closing, bird after bird. I run thru handfuls of bird seed, sunflower pips, hard corn, sprinkle it out on the sidewalk, tiny hard grains bouncing once and landing, either on cement or grass. The birds keep coming, even from high above these walks and behind roofs, sense the food, move from tree to telephone line to T.V. aerial to fence, snatch a bite, and fly back. They pour out of the sun, icy cirrus whips, birds, coming as single letters of the alphabet, and when there are twenty-six, we begin counting again and there are twenty-six more, alphabet wings, feeding and retreating, A, B, C, the beginnings of words, a single squirrel, I roll walnuts down the sidewalk, now, D, E, F, three, four, five squirrels come, out of the damp hidden bushes, take a nut in their mouths and return; the sound of walnuts landing brings squirrels from across the street and down from the trees; I run out of walnuts and begin lofting single peanuts into the direction from which each squirrel comes; the cats lie poised, watching the motion but not attacking. A single blue jay moves from tree to tree in a circle around the food; suddenly it flies down and beats a squirrel to a peanut, back thru the branches and sits high in the tree, the way some birds can pick out bright objects with which to build their nests, tinsel, and foil, and coins, and even a wrist-watch while its owner swims in the river, buried ticking in the other grasses and hays until it stops, and other birds see fish gleaming just beneath the surface of the sea, magnetic north marked by certain cracks in the land and fissures beneath the ocean, and can find their way back to the very tree where they began.

How much food is there?, how much sun poured on the earth, stored in golden jellies beneath the surface of the land? Will there be food for generations ten, a million years from now even as lizards and ferns left us our industrial coals, oils, the medium of our furnaces and cars?, and how much sun is there left?, knowing full well it will go out eventually, leaving us in the, leaving a dark smoking ash, a burnt-out corn-cob left by a squirrel just outside the corn-field fence. Every creature feeds on sun, lines its body with sun and builds its home out of stored sunlight, abandoning those that go out, crossing from pond-bed to pond, even growing legs for the journey if it has to, pursuing the dwindling Western star, migrating, emigrating, coming to a new land during the potato famine, fleeing its own slums and junkpiles, leaving its waste to the softening magic of time.

The sun itself grows legs and crawls on the earth like a fat bug, hungry for its self, cracks its own shell, eats its yolk, and in the morning rises thru

moths and fog into the corona of the Eastern sky. And how much longer
will it go on, this music?, how much food is there?, how much longer is
food possible?, is it possible to go on like this?, crowding people into the
cities where they don't fit, flushing the fruits and vegetables in, rotting thru
the night while the middleman cheats?, how much iron in the universe
that we can make soft and chew in our present form?, how many pearls
and pennies will grow again in the blueberry fields, as something we will
use?, how much time to turn a hubcap into a blackberry by the conditions
of the Stone?, before the steel flows back into the grains and the auto
graveyards become edible again?, how much real magnesium, essential
to life, except in the pawn shop?, how long will we have to wait to redeem
our present age, and the fossil fuels?, how many floating gardens of iodine,
spindles of algae to begin the chain in the muds doused with poisons from
the land, how many may-apples when the forests die before the paper on-
slaught?, how much metal if everyone wants two cars, and a car every two
years?, and how much food if the soil is drenched with smoke and the
belly filled too fast for the liver to filter?, the sewers backed up and flooding the city? How many more buffets and smorgasbords and cocktail
parties?, and grass-seed choking off the grains, and lawn-mowers crew-
cutting the landscape, trimming away the wild fruits?, how much longer
will the clouds of magi and magic hang in the morning dew, thought on
this planet, can it sustain itself?, can it find its way out of its own conscious manipulation of shape?

And what if one year the tomatoes refuse, from some inner code, to
grow? What if the cattle, tired of being food, die in the stockyards without
offspring? What if the fish die in swarms and pile up stinking on the
shores?, and all Indian prayers are forgotten?, and all Indians forbidden to
fish their waters?

What if the sun rises in a dark coat and no one knows the prayer for
removing the scab?, and this goes on day after day? Then we are changed
into something else.

Some prophesy that we are on the verge of a great famine, a dream of
seven lean cows and an abandoned ranch, corn-field without sun even
for the fungus that cysts the corn, the sunflower lacking its solar oils, the
supermarkets empty, no specials, no trading stamps; even the French restaurants closed.

But we have been alive a long time, and always on the verge of a great
famine, a black death, this is our condition, always threatened by the
occult motions of Kali beneath the city streets and beneath molecular
knowledge. We have always been at the mercy of what we cannot see.
We starved in Egypt, if Egypt was the beginning. We starved in the
Pleistocene, culling the sparse strewings of a sun that had already shone

too long, and ate berries in Siberia, and a thousand years later in the woods of Western Washington, where no human tongue had tasted ripe native fruit, and fished in frozen ocean, pulling up an alphabet, the syllables of an unknown language that lay beneath ice. There has always been an impending famine, the common people going mad and turning on each other in the frustrations of heavy bodies and stony dry earth, the priests alive, stoking certain fires, keeping their arms on the sacred drums beating out a rhythm, and the masses protest the use of foodstuff to this end, why energy wasted here when the dwindling sun should be drawn into muscles and the energies of harvest and hunt. But eventually a voice arose in the fires and they were carried South; the drums beat a path South, and all these years the old alphabet was protected, the letters kept and fed whatever sacred food could be found; they were lean, dying, almost dead, the old animals, the household words, a male and a female of each, set free finally into the new South African climate, the pluvial riverine fields, rivers opening a new country, that were once all called the Mississippi, and was the father of all waters, flooding the Natchez fields and the temples with sun, and out digestively into the swamps and ocean, the beginnings of the Maya in the Highlands, who came down into the Lowlands, strangers on the edge of their territory promising bundles of food if they would cull the jungle and complete the Aztec alphabet, drawing Q, X, R, copal, salt, rubber, S, T, U, jaguar skin, cotton, feathers, if the Egyptians would complete the great Northern alphabet, transporting ivory, ointments, slaves, oils, feathers, ostrich egg shells from the dark Southern jungles and kingdoms to the kingdom of Ur, the Northern minstrels swallowing these new suns, mu, nu, xi, the world flourishing, alphabet blown out thru shells and at the tops of winding towers, rectangles piled atop larger rectangles, dwindling into the intense chamber of the sun, the focal point from which all light and image begins.

And have always been on the verge of famine: the chicken tracks end occultly, no animal anywhere in sight, but these are their own tracks, as they walk in circles, exchanging feet, unknown markings, as though a bird flew here, or the sun walked and then returned to the sky. We have always been short of markings, clues, peats and minerals, uranium, there is a limit to fossil fuels, to New York City, but not to the land, or land itself, which must bear out the condition to which it is subject, a horror we are born to see. We have always left one field fallow, hoping to soak up the shit, the sun of our later years, all summer torpid, lying around doing nothing, praying for a miraculous rebirth, a vision.

But the original and the only source of food is sun, however packaged and arranged on the supermarket shelves, in whatever variety, no matter how late the market is open, and these eggplants and peppers heavy on

[67]

their stems can be mined only so long, canned and bottled, crated and shipped into the early urban sunlight; the farmland is taxed, and a million more children of someone come into the world. We do not, we hardly know who we are. We who have named the animals: what kind of animal? For there is another limit: it will not end until the sun ends, and we will even learn to drink pure sunlight if we have to, grow plant cells and absorb the living stream that falls on the earth's body spread to receive the impact as it always has been, become the body of the earth, filling the planet with our kind. Because we will become something yet we do not know or understand because we always have.

2

There is a discrepancy, a physical confusion: the daisy turning to rot inside, the fluids of the diseased used on the healthy, and the fluids that cause disease in the healthy used on the diseased. Day after day the hot sun. The nitrates. Our bodies are crumbling stones; our bodies pass the age of flexibility and begin to decay, even as we turn to ice; our bodies are misused by those in power, those with bodies, who think they have bodies also, our bodies . . . . The smell of shit is everywhere, the lovers farting. The smell of shit is everywhere, the cat with her nose on the squirrel's ass; the smell of shit is . . . . finally we come to love the smell of shit, and swim in the river, and melt away the twenty-six golden organic rings.

Day after day the posts hold up, the rectangles, the false geometry of the land, the chemistry blistering and stained. On the beach lie old comic books, horror stories, Flash Gordon is made to stand in a steaming hot shower, a man is seized off the street and made to lie on a bed of pins, and the bathers lie on the hot sand, covered with the ocean salt, their bodies turning tan, the metabolic sun of cancers, the thirteen year cycles of bile, the smell of liver on everything except the smell of iodine, sea-weed, the brain lying within its protective membranes, spinning with charge.

Everything is active, chemically insecure. This will end, this castle held up as though by skeletal poling, the ripe fleshy wall. It will end. It doesn't matter that it will end. There is also our time, cameo of what we are forever, not eternal life but the simple existence of a garden, a house, a kitchen, faucets leading in and out, roads, the postman stopping, a blue jay: cameo of an egg frying with bacon, of a train crossing, cameo of a grocery market, of daisies, of cats running, of cars rusting in stacks on the edge of the forest. This will end, but
not even the best of us know what this is.

Life after death, life before death, life before life and lives before and after lives. Egyptians, farmers, basketmakers, Shoshoneans. There is a disturbance in a room of mediums. Ducks. Flocks of birds. The wind. The poltergeists that chase with cats and rustle tissue paper in the closet.

Every summer we have enjoyed these walks in the woods, the river and its bright green decay of moss, the old stony chestnuts, birds and flowers. Faraway a pack of wild dogs bark; they mauled a child yesterday, blood on their teeth. The river ends in the bog, rich with snake fluids, and orchids growing up with *Typha latifolia,* the cattails. It is not a peaceful walk, is fatiguing, wearying, dizzy, without perception or interception, vast, enigmatic; we sit to read, but the ground is damp and wind blows the pages; the words are loose. There is a discrepancy here; it is not all simple, not all simply joy. The river is perhaps a happy current, but there are undercurrents, a deterioration of ikons and cameos. It is all happening here, no different than anywhere else. This is a funeral, wet and cellular, old and beginning to smell; it is our own bodies, the olfactory and visual cells wasting away, decaying in the earth. There is no reference, but a thousand sparking cross-references, intracellular, textual. I am trying to force a boat down a river, to remember the preceding instant and the next, the opening of the canal locks, and I a prisoner of circles, the compulsive ring of synapses I am electrically identified by, I continue to weave.

The grass is crushed beneath our feet, the flowers snapped. It is a lethal sun; the mint tastes of my dying body; the insects pollinate and die, three, four, each step; the cat is dead and changing under the earth; the sky is dark above the sky, and airless. The poisonous aconite swells in the green tips of the red nightshade berries. The juices grow in spring, in the liver, the medicines tuned by lunar phases. We are all one cameo, no difference between poisons and medicines, food and killing, no difference between friendly and ferocious animals. They are all medicinal, or they are all killers. What is poison is what we are made out of/bathe in/eat/ kiss/suck/fuck/discharge as symptomatic of the deeper disease, and this is nothing that SDS or the Rosicrucians can save us from though surely the latter stand a better chance. And there are verbs that command the dative, even two millenia after Roma, and the brain is stony, a reserve, the hard cell walls demanding structure, memory. The abandoned comic books are washed into the Atlantic, chambers of fish, and the text slowly removed, the cells turned back into rag, into generative grammar. We command the dative, dig a grave, the archetype, follow in a circle, yield by computer the same magical numbers, cameo of the trade route, biremes and canoes, and still the compass point turning wildly in an electromagnetic storm, the continents seeking isostasy, as they must, all this time.

The confusion is not just the cat's body altered by cold downing currents, permeating her cells as a sponge, hemorrhaging from the blow of the car, from death, which follows; the confusion is perceptually raining on the body, the head and neck dislocated as to position and alertness, constant distraction, traction, meals pouring thru, eliminated, somehow making a temple despite me, because of me, somehow a theater for dream. A tornado is sighted. I hide behind magnetic plates counting the time between. Somehow I must alert the waking cities. In this dilemma I go blind. Then the dream ends, and I too awake, the awaking cities. I am alert and hungry for breakfast again. And I'm sure coffee will move my bowels.

But one book says that the may-apple is delicious and suggests a may-apple chiffon pie, including *Podophyllum peltatum* itself, mallow plants, and graham crackers. The book on medicine reminds us that the Puritans used may-apple to heal malignant tumors, metaphysical juice passing thru the nodes. The book on poisons says to eat may-apple under no conditions. Same with marsh marigold. The book on wild foods tells us that the leaves are fine in tossed salads, while the buds can be used for canapés; they are healthy for having sucked up the rich soils that have eroded synclinal into the marsh. *Deadly Harvest* tells us that Ranunculins, including *Caltha palustris,* contain the poison protoanemonin.

But we are made of poisons, and dying by heat and sun anyway, and know it, and are our own catalysts, filling the muscles with anxiety, filling the cells with ambiguity because they are only cells, and we use them, we think, for so much more. And finally the wrong message is passed on. The phone rings in the middle of the night from a deep sleep. And we die. Poisons flow each second, must be constantly antidoted by thought, and a bedside tea, sipping the blue leaves of evening, the stars in boiling water, the Ranunculins (or the buttercup family), the catnip leaves, derivative of the mints. There was another body once. And then there was this one.

I have turned over the shit, and left the sticky parsnip flowers for the ants, and it is about to rain, and mud leaks in under the radiators covering the rugs with a thick smell, the parsnip roots on the counter, in boiling water, and it all comes back to the woman, the smell of the woman not perfumed, digestive shit beneath the perfume; our forte is not easy jest or barbecue of dead meats, summer cabanas and comedians, but we are the shit in our own locker room, and the pipes that run under the hotel and carry away the hidden desires of the guests. Our forte is not smooth speech and lyric, but the poisons which corrode language anyway, the words in punning Brownian motion, no stasis but in flux, organic chemistry, rings trading valences, oxymoron; could you tell me if you're poison before I taste you?; why don't you taste me and find out! And so what we fail to realize is that, even though this is America, this is life.

The actual mud lies beneath style, nickel-iron boiling in the earth's core and the continents still floating loosely, Pleistocene ships, hemorrhage beneath the cameo, loose electrical wires of the epileptic, hoarse sounds, the wind thru elms, the voice of all the animals at once, and we come, and are there, is the purge, spurge of the system, the biochemical resonance which is the swill, fill beneath the party, the scene beneath the mantle, and beneath clover and sorrel, the cold alchemical rain and the ball game is rained out, the cat covering its urine with dry sand, gold and brown, shifting layers of loam and time.

That even the *General Mills Cook Book* and the *Art of French Cooking* are filled with poisons and will kill us, that even below Alice B. Toklas' fowls, the rumble and pulse of servants, the actual odor of sweat and burnt burnt-out women, burnt cells in the kitchen, fabric of the meat, cells at war with cells, and there is hemorrhaging in every blackbird and cow we eat, fermentation of grapes and yeasts, wine and beer, fungicidals and preservatives, truth serums, drugs that suppress the true ailment deeper and deeper into the body, eliminating the symptoms while the poisons continue to spew, vanilla malts, gin and lime on ice, the organs numb from microbiotics, undermined at a cellular level. There are those who are gay and want to go out with cocktail glasses and toast nature, the neighbors sit with the barbecue plugged into the garage light and turning, the lamb rolled and boned, reading *Life* and *Time* and the *Ann Arbor News* while it wheels three-hundred-sixty degrees on the electric spit, releasing a smoke, the smoke passing the nostrils of the cats on the roof, into the upper trees, the yellow beetle-chewed leaves, dissolving in the upper airs (*smoak* is what we are: Paracelsus; we are the living *Evester* giving off volatile fumes all our life), the Magic Fire Charcoal Lighter, a yellow and red can, clear cameo colors, deck of playing cards spilled thru the city and each one named a street, the fumes, the lamb turning brown, the goose singing its own roasting song in *Carmina Burana*, the trick of reflexive, or disjunctive pronouns: I myself am burned: the little boy stands on the roof leaning over the roast and asks what will happen if he jumps in. "Better salt and pepper yourself first," says the neighbor, whose name is Mr. Fry, and he laughs. "What! I'll eat myself," the boy exclaims, and begins chewing on his arm.

I dreamed of a tornado last night. The winds swept the neighborhood. No one was safe. It passed overhead, higher than all the buildings, clouds, skies, touches the initial stars. We hide in the basement. We do not see.

The boy asks if he should jump into the cat's grave.

The fire burns; the rain begins; the spit is moved under the garage. The rain falls in the driveway where the mulberries are squashed by the tires.

[71]

The air is filled with smoke, cigarette deterioration of spring, name is lark, name is newport, kool, is Fabergé, Tigress, disguising odor of perfume which enables a man to dig into his origins. The body of the bird is torn apart by the cats. The littlest cat carries a crow in his mouth and runs all over the house parading it, dragging black feathers. The stench is of mud, *smoak*, perfumes, *Evester*, shampoos, old yellowing papers in the garage, scotch tape on the library books, fungus on the plum-cake, the tea drying in the laundry room, volatile mints, the sewer beneath, ashes in the furnace burned, and burned again and again, the endless metabolic heat of the house. Sewerage of animals decomposing, of lamb broiled, we are the animals we eat, in the end we are . . . . The rain is mixed with hail; a moth is batted down into a puddle, tries to fly up and is repeatedly hit. I will not be altruistic; I will not pretend. The storm drains electricity, dousing lights and candles and neurons, releasing them thru the upper air, as lightning, as radio waves, life snuffed out in water, the circuit ends, the ashes buried, the candle fumes, the cold sulphur magnesium smell of the earth pouring into our bedroom, smell of poisons we eat and manufacture ourselves, tenuous cobwebs of our time, rain on the ceiling, musk in the attic converted to salt, *mare nostrum*, our own brain, the cans of uneaten food on the shelves, the cells, the batteries preserved for later activation, salty empoisoned delicate webs. We go out driving, and the car runs on our body.

SECTION IV

HERE DANGER IS WRITTEN INDELIBLY ONTO THE TEXT

Pornography does not mean itself; it is not linear, romantic, culminative, but a form of winding tapestry; zonal, repetitive, a path of flavors thru identicals, a journey which ends in its sleepy beginnings, with no sleep in between. Pornography reveals what was hidden; then we realize it was not that that was hidden but something else. Pornography attempts to shock us, shock us sexually, but the one thing that would truly shock us is further obscured by the text.

Pornography is a tightly-wound text, a textual key to itself. It is at once a form of divination and masturbation: a person telling his own fortune stumbles on the sexuality of the Queen of Pentacles; she excites him; he leaves the ontology of the fortune and comes in her image.

Pornography is total, a world lying beneath this one like an Ice Age. The woman is in trees, in sea-water, in birds, and dead birds; her odor pours from every cottage and farm. The seeker knows what it is in his cells he must feel; he weighs every sensation in the world against this feeling; he will lock himself in a trunk if the right cells begin to tremble.

Men hang around women's clothing stores, there to divine the origin of their passion in particulars, to be excited by the particular and come to the passion no more enlightened. These purses, bras, and female cuts of cloth are not mere accessories to the fact; they are as much the cause as the body of the woman herself, if not more so in averting the passions of her own wet person; they are adored by the pornographer as direct unsocial mediants to his own act of desire.

Boys consider it a great skill to stand before images that are only remotely titillating and call up their sperm. With a luscious *Playboy* centerfold at hand, a group of boys preferred to race each other to see who could come first over a picture of Lois Lane in a Superman Comic. Pornography belongs to the imagist poets and painters (Byron, Delacroix). Each of them sought to reveal the natural world as his own delicious image, his own specific intensity of perception. They made their bowls of fruit, their odalisques, fatally desirable; this was to be their most personal vision, this least personal by-product; this was to entice others into their darkest soul.

The allure, the delight, the sense of the gourmet is in the penis (or tongue) rather than the world it tastes. Pornography is a form of endocrinomancy in which the diviner and his materia are the same subjective sensorium.

A current magazine offers us a sociology of pornography (note here that part of the delight is in disguising one's attention, i.e., to think one's self to be doing sociology and suddenly come up with a hardon). One of the points made in the article is that the author of pornography must make the book exciting in the beginning, and then have each succeeding affair more evocative, more intense than all those before it. They give us an example from a French book which is supposedly a pornographic classic. The literary climax occurs when the woman admits that she has been forced to have intercourse with a donkey by a group of bedouins. We might wish to examine the structures of this particular text:

The donkey's penis is enormous; it is the largeness of genital they seek, the penetration of our smaller order of seamed fleshy parts by a larger order represented by a giant penis, impersonally thrust, as thru the alchemical funnel. It is unsure if it is they themselves (even though men) who want to be fucked by this monster larger than all their desires, if they would like their bodies split and torn (as in war), possessed, captured, held captive (so that once, just once, the thrill itself would be equal to the promise in the pornography). The organ they would like to manipulate in minute fetiches of sight and smell and touch suddenly manipulates them, a penis so large that it can not only take responsibility for all their bizarre desires but can also take responsibility for fulfilling them. This confusion of whether they are the fucker or the fucked occurs throughout the description, is a confusion in the voice itself.

Four men hold her up to the donkey. This is intercourse with four men, the collective penis of four men's desires as though their desires spark and cause each other. They are four men bound in a single act, a single trident; their force upon the woman is one, the head of Caesar stamped on a coin, their mark left on her as the action they hold in their hands, against their own participatory weight.

Her pelvis is split and she bleeds: sadomasochism yes, but also the splitting of earth and the continents, of Geos, the woman who has lived in the old order too long and can give birth to nothing by it any more; she is torn apart; she will have children again, new children whose faces were not human in an earlier age. The penis is another order, the rhythm of the animal's thrust. In sheer biological terms it is out of joint; it is too large to fit; the forces that created penis and cunt did so in separate but homologous orders; they are ontologically discontinuous; they can come together only thru another force operating against the inherent chemicals. But that force too, remember, is born of chemicals, the same chemical universe.

It is the penis of a giant as it enters the woman's, the reader's world, not a donkey, which is where it issues from; it will not fit; four men rub grease in her cunt; it is made to fit; she is made open to visitation from a Gnostic world; she is laid open for the theosophical entry of an interceding order, space penetrated and split as a giant tree coming up thru the earth. The penetration is a phallus, indeed a fertile phallus; the penetration is between the world of animals and the cities of humans and human faces; the penetration fills the forest with animals that are neither, though they rise from the woman's spirit, her brain waves rather than her ovaries and flesh.

The woman is in their hands fully even as she is placed on the penis, held wholly and entered as a part of her at the same time; her full weight in their hands but their penises full, as though in her, metonymy allowing the body a range and duality which is beyond mortal physiology; this is what they seek, women as pocket fetishes they can pull out and fuck and put back in their pockets even as they ride on the public bus. And, of course, that no man have anymore to claim than this.

Where are the heads of these men, the four men who are the reader? Do they identify with the upper penis and thrust down into her, or do they thrust her up from below onto the penis? Do they hold a fucked woman in their hands?, or is their preference to fuck her as a giant penis while she is held?

She is too coy for them; she is a tease, a pornographic object who has titillated them for an entire book, and eluded them somehow as they lay naked and sought her in darkness behind their eyes, behind the pages of the book. And the final orgasm in such a titillating sequence must be to take the body that has been teasing the reader for so many pages, unavailable thru the mists of bad imagistic writing, unavailable essentially (as essence) and rip her open, rip her bloody with a giant cock; thus large must be the cock of the reader, having grown and grown without coming thru all these many pages, all these many books. It is an enormous summer day piling in cumulus perfumes, rolling in incompletions and lethargies without even the calm intercession of somatic cells, loose wisps of fantasies irritating the penis, women on the street, their circlets of form and smell and dress. Suddenly a *deus ex machina* cock rips it open, exposes and heals the wound; the cunt should bleed; the cock should be sore and bloody for entering too small a cunt, for attempting to enter where there is only image and no flesh, sore from enlarging on the coy, the miniscule, where all is allure and there is nothing but allure, the winding tapestry, the body cannot find the end, cannot reach inside itself to the image, cannot hold the image, firm the image, fuck the tiny inviting woman. The secrets of the body are not this easy, not this blatant; they are not reached by this convention.

The donkey attempts to rip apart the imagism, to make a definite mark on her as she aloofly sways in the offering of her body, offering it to no one. They wish to move her, leave their mark, their desire, even by a knife, a cut, by having participated in a bloody gesture of language. They have a topological problem; they wish to touch her insides when she is inside them; they wish to give their inward cells some outward resolve in further

[77]

patterns of internality. They can find no outward; they are hopelessly wound in the cells that respond inward; in these passages they wander looking for what they will recognize as something else.

When the donkey comes it is as the reader comes: darkly, with no perception of the strange order into which four sadomasochistic men nonetheless hold its penis; they are moved beyond understanding yet they have entrusted their sacred organs to these imagists, these pornographic authors. They do not know where their penises are, and the book gives no help; they put down the book and masturbate for direction, and they are sore, and they do not know if they are the donkey or the woman or the men holding the woman, and if when they come they must grow weak and drop her. They are in a secret world, a world of possible magic, but the way in which they have entered has closed the secrets of this world and their bodies to them. They are surrounded by mysteries but their perceptual field dwells on the banal. They come in that darkness, and do not know where, or why the sperm goes where it does except that its stain is the only mark they have left on the physical world. They do not know where of image and where of flesh; they do not feel the dynamics of penetration and the static of ascending orders; they are dark and dumb and stand in the sunlight; they stand there unwilling to move, to be moved; they are susceptible; four men come holding the woman of another species, perhaps their own species; she is also perhaps an angel, a supernal as well as a famous whore; she is tiny but she is whole. They see her there, they know they must respond. They know the possibility, even in their remotest senses, of infinite magic and surcease from pain. The penis enters anyway, as it must even into the angel, into the bed-clothes of sleep, cell-walls of dream; the human possibilities are infinite, the possibilities of the angels who guard men and cannot be touched except in sacrament (and the sacrament of sex). But it comes in the darkness of its own limited flesh.

2

The Hurons destroy their Iroquois prisoner organ by organ, with clubs, and fires, and sharp points. His limbs are removed singly; he is kept alive to see the sun, or have the sun see him. He is made to sing a song of himself, and he sings it before and during the torture.

"Before he was brought in, the Captain Aenons encouraged all to do their duty, representing to them the importance of this act, which was viewed, he said, by the Sun and by the God of war. He ordered that at first they should burn only his legs, so that he might hold out until daybreak . . . ."

The more boisterous torturers are restrained; he is kept alive without limbs; every portion of his body is touched at least once by the firebrand. It is essential that he see the morning sun. It is essential to mutilate the body while consciousness still inhabits there, to receive feedback as to the effects of such colossal acts. Consciousness howls back; it is the hysterical but formal singing of the captive.

"The cries redoubled at his arrival; he is made to sit down upon a mat, his hands are bound, then he rises and makes a tour of the cabin singing and dancing; no one burns him this time, but also this is the limit of his rest—one can hardly tell what he will endure up to the time when they cut off his head."

These events take place in the cabin of the great war Captain; it is a men's house; no women are allowed. The victim is a man, an Iroquois warrior; he is attacked by men; he is driven to beyond his own control, breathless, outside of feeling, of passion; he is the total account of their brutality, their own wild passion.

"After this each one armed himself with a brand, or a piece of burning bark, and he began to walk, or rather to run, around the fires; each one struggled to burn him as he passed. Meanwhile, he shrieked like a lost soul; the whole crowd imitated his cries, or rather smothered them with horrible shouts."

He is wounded into a woman, a woman who is a man and cannot be fucked conventionally, who is wounded into another sort of concavity, his organs opened and burned soft into the reverse sensual charge, his closed flesh slit into a vagina, a thousand clitorises cut loose, driven into sensitivity of the male weight; the body is unmaled, the hardness torn off; it is made responsive to clubs and fire brands; the men drive this former man to an unheard of passion, a passion that is the collective representation of all their male ferocity, all their power in sex and in war; the formal account of this passion is released in the victim's song; they are good lovers, they have touched him deep and he has not yet died.

"The whole cabin appeared as if on fire; and, athwart the flames and dense smoke that issued therefrom, these barbarians—crowding one upon the other, howling at the top of their voices, with firebrands in their hands, their eyes flashing with rage and fury—seemed like so many demons who would give no respite to this poor wretch. They often stopped him at the other end of the cabin, some of them taking his hands and breaking the bones thereof by sheer force; others pierced his ears with sticks which they left in them; others bound his wrists with cords which they tied roughly, pulling at each end of the cord with all their might. Did he make the round and pause for a little breath, he was made to repose upon hot ashes and burning coals . . . ."

[79]

This description, by Le Jeune (1637), appears in the *Jesuit Relations*. The sense, apparent though not manifest, in the account is of the victim willingly participating in the orgy. He sings his song, parades sexually in full male blood before the armed warriors; he announces himself as their fresh meat, their male block out of which to carve a woman. All thru the torture he is called upon to sing his song, and he does so with remarkable strength.

"At the end of an hour he began to revive a little, and to open his eyes; he was forthwith commanded to sing. He did this at first in a broken and, as it were, dying voice; but finally he sang so loud that he could be heard outside the cabin. The youth assembled again; they talk to him, they make him sit up—in a word they begin to act worse than before. For me to describe in detail all he endured during the rest of the night, would be impossible; we suffered enough in forcing ourselves to see a part of it . . . ."

The Jesuit is perhaps squeamish in describing the blatant sexuality of the torture, though the conventional aspects of fire and brimstone, and Hell, are depicted in full Biblical narrative. There is a precedent for sadism and pain in the Bible, a precedent even for damned unbaptized souls on earth to act out, unconsciously, the very intaglio of Hell. But the sexual torture is mentioned nowhere in the Bible; there are other precedents for this torment, not that "in a word they begin to act worse than before," but that they pursue their actions to a natural consequence.

The male is made into the female.

The female in the male is revealed.

An ambiguous mixture of chromosomes: XXY.

There are vestigial breasts on the male, and the clitoris is called "the little penis." Roheim, among others, has described the subincision rites of the Australian Aborigines (whereby a slit is made in the male erogenous zone) a gaining by the male of the vagina, and hence the full sexual ambiguity and fertility of the world. Coyote, as trickster in Northwest Coast Amerindian myths, is famous for removing his penis and having subsequent intercourse with a prominent male of the tribe; he is made pregnant and gives birth to royal children. He also propels his unattached penis across the lake to impregnate the princess who is bathing. Theoretically it is possible for him to do both these things at the same time, thereby describing, in the medium of his very person, the continuous ambiguity of male and female desires, and male and female inheritance, and ambiguous inheritance, as male thru female (in the avunculocal situation), and boys from their mothers and paternal aunts. Males and females exist in the same families, in the same clans; male and female desires for each other are not totally separate and complementary; they overlap. A recurrent dream is the one in which a best friend becomes a girl and the dreamer fucks him, the penis clearly passing into the vagina; what would seem to be inalterable in his waking mind becomes so easily pliable in the dream state. He awakes, not so much amazed that it happened as that it happened without confusion and without question; it is hardly the typical homosexual dream. In other variants of this, one's wife becomes his husband and she fucks him, or she dreams of organically having the penis and entering him. Often there may be a dream of a third sex, a person played by either a boy or a girl who is simultaneously married to the members of a couple at the same time they are married to each other.

The sexuality present in ambiguity is a different form of emotion; it is passionate, oriented in the erogenous zones, and yet different than the desire of the male for the female and the female for the male. It is a desire that has given up hope of clarification and pure Christian, or even Qabbalistic, love; it is a desire that has become suffused in exploiting the confusions, that seeks its generation in a tension between poles. The human condition, which is ambiguous, frightening, and strange, is conjoined with the sexual condition, which is equally ambiguous, frightening, strange, and seductive, and neither is a lesser subset of the other. These men and women, thus possessed, seek more than sexual affirmation in the sexual act; they seek affirmation of the total condition of life in sex, and affirmation of sex in every other aspect of life; finally the two are inseparable. Stimulation, as always, is brought about by tricks, snares, lures; interwound circles and sinuosities are the means for attracting partners, as the winding circles and arcs are tattoed on the body either to their own alluring end, or as a simultaneous description of the social and physical movements of the body prior to the act. All direction is indirection; the body would respond no other way, experiencing such as the basic liquidity of itself.

Lévi-Strauss describes certain aspects of this in his essay called "The Art of Asia and America":

"Caduveo art carries the dislocation process both further than, yet not as far as, Northwest Coast art. It does not carry it as far, because the face or body on which the artist works is a flesh-and-bone face and body, which cannot be taken apart and put together again. The integrity of the real face is thus respected, but it is dislocated just the same by the systematic asymmetry by means of which its natural harmony is denied on behalf of the artificial harmony of the painting. But since this painting, instead of representing the image of a deformed face, actually deforms a real face, the dislocation goes further than in the case previously described. The dislocation here involves, besides the decorative value, a subtle element of sadism, which at least partly explains why the erotic appeal of Caduveo women (expressed in the paintings) formerly attracted outlaws and adventurers toward the shores of the Paraguay River. Several of these now aging men, who inter-married with the natives, described to me with quivering emotion the nude bodies of adolescent girls completely covered with interlacings and arabesques of a perverse subtlety."

Hence the confusion of the yet-to-be American Revolution presents a stage for the men to be women and the women to be men. But, even as the changing of histories and structures, the situation is more ambiguous and contradictory than this. Men and women both dress in revolutionary clothes; they fight side-by-side; they make love in the foxholes and in the evenings between battles (Margaret Randall and Diane Di Prima); the soldiers are not distinguished in their genders; the army is no longer homosexual; the soldiers are prepared to occupy, of their own numbers, the land which they conquer. At the same time, however, in this particular brand of poetry, the man is used poetically much as the woman has previously been used. The moon-goddess-whore of the male poets is suddenly complemented by the Guevara-Ammon-Ra-Revolutionary of the female poets. The man is non-individual; he carries a gun; he takes target practice outside the city; he shoots at the fascist cops; he is Apollo, figure worthy of the whore-girl-soldier's love after the battle. But he is also wounded, as the Iroquois captive; women are warned:

> "(not to freak out
> at the sight of torn or half-cooked flesh) . . ."

The war is the ambiguity of social and political relations, is the ambiguous stage on which the male and female drama is enacted. Did these women ever want men?, or themselves as men? In the midst of more publicized revolution the secret war between the sexes has been going on for millenia, the battle of either to uncover the other in themselves, to do without the other, to submerge themselves in the attraction of the other, to heal platonically the division between male and female, rich and poor, saved and damned, alive and dead, which has kept mankind in sadistic agony for all its time, and the full lifetime of individuals. A thousand poetic schemes are offered to heal the divisions, to make us one, so that the lover in his bed can finally breathe easily, unthreatened from the outside and unthreatened in his soul, so that he can finally be free of Huron Indian torture and germ warfare, and ambiguous success, so he can finally love with his full body all that he loves, and no longer doubt the condition which brings him here (but it is always in doubt, and the sexual dialectic is the same as the political one: let us change this world, as men and women; let us finally be happy, the men quavering before their Caduveo oppressors, Allen Ginsberg shaking in the gymnasium before the machinery of another angel, Kenneth Anger's motorcyclist rubbed with mustard, and innumerable alleyway rapes of young girls, virgins, that the only relief from pain, the only successful strategy is to enter the world like a god, like an intruder, superman with a super-cock, machine gun loaded with bullets, that in a world where cruelty is a possibility, to be cruel is sometimes the only solution).

But even the protagonist acts with ambiguity; the passion for the ambiguous is ambiguous itself, and so on. Perhaps one Huron might wish to relieve his flesh by rescuing the Iroquois and nursing him to health; perhaps the rapist seizes only so that the girl can be brought back from the darkness of himself, can be soothed by someone else. And the man who leaves bombs on the subway merely wishes to alert the human race to this ambiguity within itself, that such a thing can be done, and has been, and the motive, inexplicable as the act is unexpected, is the sheer exploitation of an unexpected world that rides visibly alongside this one, the spear violating the ear-drum, the knife-blade cutting thru the eye.

There are those who wonder even about the fact that this world is based on destroying and eating life, the herbivore chewing plants, the carnivores killing the herbivores and cruelly tearing them apart, as the lion rips apart a deer, or the shark a small fat fish. These food chains are unavoidable, are the continuous means of our own survival; the knife lingers deep in our racial memory of teeth and claws; even as Jainists we cannot escape the consequences of what we kill.

Early in his novel *World Enough and Time* Robert Penn Warren desribes those fantasies of his main character that come from reading the Bible:

"Here over and over again was the story of the one against the many, some stubborn, hard-headed and hard-handed peasant or villager, some preacher sour in pride and righteousness, or some ecstatic female who would take the rack or the flame before the authority of the received opinion. There were pictures here. One in particular he returned to in the end, the picture of a young woman tied cruelly to a post 'so that the bonds seemed to crush her sweet flesh and her face lifted up while the flames rose about her.' He poured for hours over that picture, which we can visualize as crude, blurred, and splotched on the spongy paper of the ruined book. 'Sometimes looking fixedly upon it, my breath almost stopped and my bowels turned to water. Sometimes the strange fancy took me that I might seize her from the flame and escape with her from all the people who crowded about for her death. At other times it seemed that I might throw myself into the fire to perish with her for the very joy. And again, my heart leaping suddenly like a fish and my muscles tight as at the moment when you wait to start a race, I saw her standing there bound, with no fire set, and I myself flung the first flaming faggot and could not wait to see her twist and strive against the tight bond in the

[83]

great heat and toss her head with the hair falling loose to utter a cry for the first agony!'"

The Iroquois stands before his captors; he is no longer an Iroquois; he is already dead. The Iroquois is no longer an Iroquois; his tribe mourns his death; his widow is given another from his family; he is already dead. He exists only long enough to leave his body to these experimenters; it is not their experiment alone; it is an experiment in which he too had a life-long interest; now he is just as willing as they to have his body be the object of the test. He gives it to them because he has already abandoned it; they keep him awake in death long enough to see the results also; he is allowed to see his body shaped into a woman beneath their delicate tools; he sings the critical description as he is told to, or tells his body to; he does not protest the pain because he is already dead; already another has taken his place; already another is sleeping with his wife. He protests no more than the dead man protests the instantaneous heat of centuries, the forms and bacteria gobbling up the body he once used; he is raped; his death is transformed into life; he is brought back from the dead to the living as a woman; he willingly complies. He is allowed to remain conscious during this transmigration; he is dead for an hour, having fainted; he awakes and sees the sunlight again; it is no longer the same world; it is another world (as it is another body) into which he has been brought. He must describe to them this different world (his song at daybreak is for that purpose); he must sing them the song of the sunlight perceived by a man whom they have turned into a woman. Not only is his maleness quenched, but his and their longing for femaleness.

And no woman is allowed into the great war Captain's house.

✦   ✦   ✦   ✦   ✦

Diane Di Prima tells us the same thing: that it is not the life or the individual vision worth saving, but the collective vision which rules over all. Continuous political and sexual revolution must be fomented; war captives cannot be put to death instantly or set free: there is a game that must be played for keeps; every move is important; every move has meaning; every move must uphold and advance danger and ambiguity, whence the full possible sexual exhilaration is generated. Without such games we would be weak pawns of an illusory order. The strangeness of human life is proclaimed and celebrated by its strangeness.

She writes:

> "The value of an individual life, a credo they taught us
> to instill fear, and inaction, 'you only live once'
> a frog in our eyes, we are
> endless as the sea, not separate, we die

[84]

a million times a day, we are born
a million times, each life and death . . . ."

Hence the Iroquois is sacrificed to ambiguity and cruelty; his place is already taken by another man, one just like himself, perhaps even his brother. For every girl raped there is one who is not raped, or more than one, and more than one sodomist for every rapist, and so on. Hordes upon hordes of individual soldiers are told to give their lives in kamikaze (the divine wind of genetic surplus). The burden of the moral decision, the specific poem is taken from the individual and given back to the governing body, the full array of soldiers and guerrilla judges. Does the end justify the means?

"Tribe
an organism, one flesh, breathing joy as the stars
breathe destiny down on us, get
going, join hands, see to business, thousands of sons
will see to it when you fall, you will grow
a thousand times in the bellies of your sisters."

No.

We are not this wise. Or wise in this way. This is merely a social ruse to keep the tribe going, as the Iroquois provide another husband. Our deaths are sustained by what our lives were, but not in what happens afterward, for once we are dead (and even before) this has happened. The Revolution will no more heal the human ambiguity than the doings in the whore-house, or in the cabin of the great war Captain. The Great War goes on. The kamikazes do not give their lives in vain, and this they realize in the completeness of a simultaneously previous and subsequent life. But to the opposing nation, the suicide squads have succumbed to a fatal ruse, the same fatal ruse that both sides have succumbed to. The world goes on; ambiguity is not healed; the war goes on; the rapes continue; the Hurons are dead but their tortures are alive. The kamikaze heals his own sexual confusion, but the revolution leaves the country just as before. The ambiguity is the eternal form of the life; our lives are made up of resolving it. Perhaps there is another way.

3

Each creature is cut to a single possible life, as a chess piece. The squirrel chitters, flaps its red tail at the dog; and the sharpened claw of the cat slices open the fat quail. These are the remaining students of an ancient genetic training, whose education is ruthless, fixed, whose ethics could only be transmigration. They wear the uniforms of different armies, but the flesh is the same, and they share this motive: the breaking of karma, whose turn locks them indelibly in their given fur.

They move not because, but because they are limited, these walruses and vicars and swains. And the ancient and most royal game is played, chivalrous yes, illegal always illegal murder, so that the cats do not even know what to do with these snouty field-mice whose necks they have broken in play. Only the nitrogen cycle dismembers and hides the shamed corpse, and in the one place it can never be found.

In theosophical vision, man alone walked out of the macrocosm perfected of the symmetrical operation, and became the lighthouse keeper, chained as he was to a Crow or Duck Island, one piece of rocky body beyond which he could not trespass, even if he did. And he did.

The animals come from imperfect matings, rapes, perversions. So was the Qabbalogram snapped by diminishing exponents, that once the most regular of all fluid objects, and the stars were joined by astrals in the lower heavens.

The animals are people and the people are animals: the Chicago Cubs, the Black Panthers, the totemic child with a rabbit's head and swift back legs. Here in the threshold where man and beast are indistinguishable, the conquistadors ride high on each other's unexplored organs: the australopithecines galloping into a herd of ancestral pigs, throwing stones, the first days of Bob Feller's career.

The animals, being different from each other, mark the differences between people, as between types of lovers and corporations and practical jokers. Some animals are passionate lionlike lovers; Leigh Hunt says that fish are "Legless, unloving, infamously chaste." Animals are the geomantic signs by which our world is made habitable, our nouns tilled and fertilized; they live in a different land and train our priests and magicians—and their extinction will leave us without a language, without an alphabet of genes in which to talk of protein and life. When we shall flee from the forest fire it will be together, locked in our costumes, deer and chipmunks, carpenters, kings, beavers, electricians, but no men.

SECTION V

ON EATING AND BEING EATEN

1

We are all self-seeking. We seek ourselves as the lizard seeks the moon, tide-water on his back. We seek what we are, everywhere in the world. We seek the key to an energy which possesses us and drives us on, and in seeking it we are the energy. We break on earth as moisture; we break with electricity on the outer worlds.

And Io pounds Jovian sleep. The radio telescope snoozes in the quiet sun, a noisier star exploding with history at its flayed edge. An anthropologist studies the Jivaro Indians, why they see the wet jungles as an illusion, the warm dream world as their given life. An astronomer is writing his thesis on the eccentricities in Pluto's orbit. A biologist studies taste distinction in insects. A crytallographer observes the life-currents of stone.

And the ship moves. And the moon moves. And magnetism moves. And tastes change. Dress styles go up and down, a biologic snake of values. The politician speaks to small Ohio towns from the back car of his train. The St. Louis Cardinals play baseball in Japan; It has secretly changed into another game; statistics break the dam and flow out into the Third World Sea. We must know what to do with what happens to us, keep it what it is before it changes into some lesser thing. Denny McClain didn't know what to do with 31 wins; he confused it with an organ and Las Vegas. And so the Sirens lure the true lover from his wife by fantasy, and he dies with less than when he began, broken, desiring what he had, the divorce final as the new phase of the moon.

Osiris rises with uplifted arms; Osiris sinks into the tombs of Egypt, casting his orange message on the hills and the junk river. Brown blood fills the sky, and the body of a strange frog is washed up on shore. Onassis marries Jackie Kennedy; the hexagram is closed. We have been on the earth since the beginning and yet we do not understand, even hear, the music when it plays, calls to us. We have been here as carbon, as pre-carbon, we have been here as electrics and flames and flesh; the royal marriage burns in the archegonium; a brown menstrual blood floods the Polynesian village, killing all the red fish. The Nootka chief is buried in a totem pole. In the Mary Worth series a mother seduces her daughter's boy-friend to show her what a two-timer he is. She says:

Onassis takes his wife to a secret island. The Kwakiutl totem pole is the morning newspaper, tells how the chief made the Russian missionaries eat shit. We are all self-seeking. What we seek is what we know is ourselves. The Prince inherits a prison; the turtle lays his eggs; Jackie Onassis: seek completion of the system, which itself is limited, as marriage possibilities in an aristocracy. Pluto moves in an eccentric orbit, the sun a distant Christmas star. A megalith is found on the moon; Elliot Smith sees its origins in Egypt, passage out thru Indonesia, Mississippi, lower delta Mars. The quasar calls out its name in energy and splayed patterns; the queen calls out her name by marriage, by 13 moons held in crisscrossing orbits. The solar wind combs the comet's hair. In the picture above the mother is still wearing the gown in which she seduced Johnny Mateo, her daughter's rotten lover; the lights were thrown on; they were embracing on a couch; now Johnny is gone and the daughter is in bed; the role has changed; the aspect of deity is different; she is still wearing the transparent gown. So the Marsupial; so Stonehenge; and Saturn with its rings; so the glacial moraine of France and Nebraska; the planet Venus, its perfumes and veils, which have become its mysterious clouds.

We seek what we are, to break this topologic ring around our heads ("Will the circle be unbroken/By and by, Lord, by and by!"); we seek ourselves in hysteria, madness, anger, in rigid social systems and winter cold medicines; we seek a resonance ringing with our own order, a resonance whose lowest unit of climb is ourselves.

An animal fills the chemical conditions of its shape (amoeba, starfish, beaver), guards its territory, fucks, kills, buries, gives birth, and defends its young, fills its own emblematic Blakean seal. The cat purrs, resonant with Mars. The baboons race across the prairie; meteors sink in the cold night. We seek an animal identity, a complex series of transforming signs and emblems by which we are what we are, and from which nothing else can be derived. Here we lie secure, nursing our planets, our comet tails, sucking the end of our nutrition, our dream. We are not one beast; we are not even an imaginary compound beast like the pegasus or the wasgo (a Haida beast composed of wolf and whale). We are a thousand beasts with a thousand feathers, a thousand constellar holes in the sky crying out for a single resonant hoot.

We are all self-seeking because there is nothing else possible; it all begins with us, begins here, and everything we do is part of our syntax, the symptomology of our heat. We are self-seeking and everything ends in a ring: the world of telecommunications, age of discovery, Arunta and Arapaho, Spice Islands, Moon and Arctic, ocean and cell, photomicrograph and Miró, map of Mars and electrical map of the United States, Polynesian taboo and Biblical taboo, totems and totem poles and Freud and Navaho doctors and Lévi-Strauss, quantum mechanics and projective verse, Einstein as the Delphic Oracle, giving advice to the love-lorn, his brain given to science, moon-map on sale, Blake's flowers and the Linnaean system of worms and floods, isostasy of earth and Sufi dancer; a topologic ring closes in the earth, a dictionary, A - Zymurgy, a basket of pine cones and marsh marigold buds served as canapés, a tea of apples and rose hips, a red yew-berry chewed by the hungry squirrel; each act completes the system; the Sphynx electrocutes; the riddle is solved each instant, and each instant generates itself in a new form. Doesn't the mother wonder who her daughter will date next, what we will find in the cell, on the moon, how we will feed the starving millions now that we have cured one sick cat? All exploration turns back to us, as Blake's creatures cry out from beneath the microscope, that they are and that he give them life. Everything in the creation is linked to us, a soft membrane, correlate point for every star and star-system, every species and subspecies; every geologic map is a map of our neural passages; every river carries holy blood, is veins; every voyage, leaving here, at the queen's court, returns here, even if passing clear around the world ocean, the galaxy, even if laden with gold, natives, and exotica, even if the ship is as large as a continent, or a planet, returns to the initial port of call. The Qabbala is our nickel-iron core; we are the nickel-iron core, and the Qabbala is the universe; a man with his arms stretched out touches all visceral organs, is a map of his digestive, circulatory, nervous, endocrine, and reproductive systems, his solar system, is a map of the universe, touches all distal points, all electrons, all bodies even light years away. Touch is merely touch. The universe crumbles at the magnetism like a sympathetic ginger.

We are self-seeking: feed the squirrel a nut, watch him break it open; he is not a person; he is not as well-fed; he cracks the nut with his front teeth, rolls its surface thru paws; he is a squirrel; he returns to the tree; a cold winter is coming; he buries half the nuts; is there a map of our front yard on his brain?; his life is shorter than ours, but this is no difference either here or there; a year in Mercury's hot metabolism takes only 88 days; Pluto's year is 248 years of Earth history; there is no difference here or there; the squirrel has a tiny penis; standing on his hind legs seems a homunculus, a little man; and he as we, or we as he, can escape only to the same points, can flee only across the same holy paths, can pray only in the same temple of fur and flesh; we seek ourselves in him, feed him a part of ourselves, feed him from our closed economy; the yew-berry, the mulberry, the horse chestnut he gets on his own; he is cut to the same conditions we are, cut in the same precise limitations, incised shape, rhythmic, metabolic, almost-molten life; there is no star that es-

[91]

capes these conditions nor any beast that escapes these locked stars, these dark homosexuals moving thru political meetings asking, "You want to fuck?"; we are no better off than the squirrel, no worse off either; we are not any better filled with steak than he is with nuts; Onassis is not better filled by his island than the squirrel is king over his territory, as the squirrel, penis of quicksilver, fucks the dominant female, his queen, in the tree; we tolerate what we are (as he does); we throw him nuts, but there is no break in the system, no universe between us giving from the grocery store and him receiving from the open animistic world; there is no altruism either; we are self-seeking; and one day we will both sip from goblets of pure sun, the world's carnivorous oecology closing on an elemental feast; even the cold stones will feed on their favorite biscuits of light; we stand before the mirror, before the squirrel; he is a homunculus, a dwarf; he is a shipping magnate, a peanut-eater; he is Johnny Mateo, driven chittering from the nest; we stand in the mirror of our own reflected dwarf-self; we throw the nut; we seek the closing of the system, the closing of sight, of touch, of taste, his little paw laid for balance on my thumb as he takes the nut, turns, and flees back into the mirror; we are part of one unbroken non-altruistic oecological system; we are closed like the planets and moons to smaller and smaller rings, smaller and smaller orbits, smaller diets and shorter lives, chiromancy of the wedding ceremony, of Kepler's orbits, of Newton seeking the hum and color of God; the squirrel takes the nut and turns; the king takes the queen from another country, another dynasty; the ships filled with wealth pass as single countries on the open seas; the astronaut rings the whole earth in the smaller orbit of his brain; on the book-shelves manifold galaxies and dimensions of science fiction, a universe bursts from this single wellspring planet, a mythology unlocked from the letters of the alphabet; we go on day after day with nothing else to do but stare in the mirror and watch, and sometimes the squirrel is the mirror; we sit and look out the window, to what we are, and sense within, to what we are; the squirrel, what he is, sits just outside the window, plucking the yew bush free of seeds; we look out the window into a mirror, and there is no escape, not even at the distance of Pluto, not even in throwing the squirrel peanuts from the dominion of the roof where we sit reading in books the story of him and us, and our planet and its sounds; this is the horror, but this is the happiness too; there is no way out; there will be nothing better, but there will be nothing worse; and as deep as it goes we have the power to go, even in our thoughts; the American space program is for naught in Blake's system but serves to farm the moon under glass domes and collect clear pools of cosmic food; there is nothing outside the system; there is nothing in the system that can be ignored; the prisons are not separate from the society, they are part of it; and Mary Shelley's Frankenstein is part of us, is not separate from our lives, nor is the squirrel's winter, which we do not enter by sympathy though there we enter our own cold winter of Indo-European time; the worst we imagine is in fact true; but so is the best we imagine; everything has meaning or nothing has meaning, the lizard's thoughts, the geology of the moon, the band-work on a piece of gneiss, the eccentricities of Pluto's orbit, the taste patterns of bees, the flight of sea-gulls, the Jet-Oiler football score in the pouring rain, a Mary Worth cartoon strip, the New York *Times* magazine section bra ads, the reproduction of the starfish, the making of Hopi prayer-sticks and Tsimshian dyes, the engraving on Mayan coins; everything has meaning, is closed in its meaning; the system closes, holding all its beings in. We are given a deck of cards; one card is the squid; one card is the mythical being who inhabits Antares and all its planets; one card is Bottom and Titania; one card is the television funeral; one card is the television wedding, a card of love potions, donkey's heads, Johnny Johnson singing to the Statue of Liberty, and a woman who thinks she is Jackie Kennedy; one card is Vic Raschi during his best year; one card is the skee-ball game, an orange ball in the twenty-point ring; one card is the fiddler crab; one card is the red flamingo; one card is Schiapparelli looking at Martian canals; one card is the cat-and-dog flea; one card is the Russian map of the dark side of the moon; one card is a mirror, and thru it is shuffled the whole genetic deck; we think we see everything; we think we see the man-apes of Africa; we think we see the rain on a Mediaeval city; we think we see the woman in the courtyard taking a shower in her pink bathroom, a star lit on dark brick; the cards shuffle so rapidly they become water, our own face reflected back, a man with a squirrel's head, a squirrel begging, he has the face of Henry VIII, and a crown on his head.

2

There would seem to be an endless supply of salmon and the Bella Coola pull them in by the hundreds during the mating season, enough fish for feasting and exchange. And though the pink flesh is baked and eaten, the skeleton is returned to the returning river.

For the fish are a tribe living at the source of the waters. In their own ceremonial times they put on red fish costumes and swim against the water, appearing in broad inland daylight as pure fish. Here they may be eaten as flesh, their costumes indistinguishable from what they are made of, what nourishes the Bella Coola. They are plentiful, and there is but one requirement: that the entire skeleton be returned whole to the river, these to float back to the source, pulled by moon and current, these to rejoin their tribe at the end of the ceremony, wasted and wan, their ceremonial clothing consumed by the dance. They redon their human flesh, but if any part of the skeleton is not returned, that persons will be missing an arm or a leg, even a head, and in reprisal the fish will be forbidden to return upstream. This is conservation, unconscious, indirect, that the Bella Coola must avoid polluted streams flowing between two lands, avoid polluting the stream into the supernatural. This is a serious business, for the city makes no food, makes only revolution, and lives off the country. The Bella Coola return these bodies to the sea because food in the world is scarce, always has been, too long, too many years to wait for the bodies of the dead to return. "We do not wish to starve."

So in his article on sanctity and adaption, Rappaport cites two essential tautologies: that every living being is connected to every other living being, and that the environment is so complex that we cannot predict the total consequences of any action. So the supernatural world, in which all beings, visible and invisible, are connected by the great spiritual thread, in which the consequences are never seen yet always critical, is not just similar but identical to the natural world. It is science which operates with an imaginary environment, an environment it imagines it can control, in which it believes its own predictions, setting limits on just how far it will trace a poison or follow a river. Who cares if insecticide in Iowa pollutes the Great Lakes, who cares if the poisonous wastes from the potato factory in Maine pour into New Brunswick, as long as the crud passes political boundaries? Who cares if the microorganisms are poisoned, the algae and snails choked, these are not men's delicacies? Who cares about the supernatural, the world we cannot see? Who cares what happens to the skeletons of the fish after the fish are eaten, when every house has a garbage disposal; except during a garbage strike in New York the people forget that there is waste and the waste goes somewhere, motorboats killing off everything in a lake during successive Memorial Days and July 4's and Labor Days? And every living organism shares in the consequences, and the consequences are collective, only civil wars says the astronaut looking down at Earth, only civil wars even as the hunter downs the bear, the fish are caught in the Bella Coola trap. And everyone is simultaneously the benefactor and the victim; we are all victimized by what we are made out of, by, in fact, that we are made out of anything. The consequences never cease but pass and rebound, and this is the story of light in the universe, a sun whose powers flood on beyond Earth, beyond planets, an Earth which receives the decay of other stars.

Those peoples who treat the environment like a sacred text, who fear the consequences of blind and obsessive actions, reap what would appear to be the benefits of the supernatural and are at least the benefits of the complex web of interpenetrating causes and effects in which they are actively lodged: the return of scarce and seasonal resources, of the ancestral geese each spring. No living being is to be harmed in some cults; in others nothing is killed without propitiation, no plant or feather plucked without concern, and prayer. And we, as Rappaport points out, are a people to whom what is sacred is: "What's good for General Motors is good for the nation." Advertising logos, pastoral singsong and Salem-choked countrysides, Ben Franklin maxims and hoarding pennies and dry goods in fallout shelters, stealing behind the employer's back so that sometimes the meat leaves the restaurant without even being unwrapped.

This nation scorns the invisible, but the invisible consequences pursue it to the grave. Without a supernatural we are losing what is . . . . natural, destroying our lands, with no concern for what we cannot see: the ends of river systems, the chemistry of marshes, the roots beneath the earth, the beginnings of food chains in the microcosm, the sea. DDT overkill: leaving not even enough bees to pollinate our flowers, enough stomach parasites to digest the foods we swallow.

For in the end it is clear that sanctity, the salvation of individual souls, or those things called the conscious arm of God's work, are simultaneously the good of our land and our existence, and in fact we cannot distinguish one mission of salvation from another, the farmer from the priest from the beaver shitting in the lake. Christian alchemy supercedes Christianity here, for Earth is the alchemical test of its metals, silver and gold and chlorophyll, and the delicate metaphors of ecological balance and chemical changes behind which lies the key to the fact that anything is at all.

"Too much thought only leads to trouble. All this that we are talking about now happened in a time so far back that there was no time at all. We Eskimos do not concern ourselves with solving all riddes. We repeat the old stories in the way they were told to us and with words we ourselves remember. And if there should then seem to be a lack of reason in the story as a whole, there is yet enough remaining in the way of incomprehensible happenings, which our thought cannot grasp. If it were but everyday ordinary things, there should be nothing to believe in. How came all the living creatures on earth from the beginning? Can anyone explain that? . . . . You talk about the stormy petrel catching seals before there were any seals. But even if we managed to settle this point so that all worked out as it should, there would still be more than enough remaining which we cannot explain. Can you tell me where the mother of the caribou got her breeches from; breeches made of caribou skin before she had made any caribou? You always want these supernatural things to make sense, but we do not bother about that. We are content not to understand."

We are made of flesh and we eat flesh. We pretend to erect boundaries between ourselves and the animals, our food, ring them with taboos and diminutives, yet all the time we eat from our own body, and the drain is evident, the loss is absolute; we wear down; after a certain age we stop growing, we must be worn. We are cast in a paradox, in a mirror. We are lost in a desert, and it is our own ratio which repeats, nothing alien. "Water, water, everywhere, but not a drop to drink." Because all water is polluted because all water is living because all protoplasm is stolen from life, to feed life. Because every animal is ambiguous because every animal is almost human. Because every human being is an animal. The Talmud: avoid those beasts which mix parts: shellfish, pigs, mice, camels, hares, rock badgers, chameleons, moles, crocodiles. But how can we tell the parts which are not mixed, the animals from the beginning adapted to God's kingdom and not the microniches of this world? How is anything kosher, unmixed with everything else? When milk and meat are the complements of mammalian existence?

We are not separate from the universe. We cannot arbitrate its matters as calm judges. We eat. Never let that be forgotten. We kill the very mother goose to whom we have given our name. We bind ourselves by formal ties to a world from which we are never separate anyway.

Ivaluardjuk, the Eskimo shaman, takes up our theme:

"The greatest peril of life lies in the fact that human food consists entirely of souls.

"All the creatures that we have to kill and eat, all those that we have to strike down and destroy to make clothes for ourselves, have souls, like we have, souls that do not perish with the body, and which must therefore be propitiated lest they should revenge themselves on us for taking away their bodies."

3

We return now to the fish market; it is late in the day, and the proprietor is about to close. "A pound of Coho salmon and a box of whale steak." He chops, pulls apart, and weighs; Libra balances the price. Now we ask him if he has any leftover scraps from his choppings that our cats can have, bits and pieces of stars and intestines. "Man, I'm about to throw out fifty fish that won't keep till tomorrow." He picks them up by the

[96]

armful and fills a cellophane sack with them: all specific fish, with the eyes of i-dentity, wrapped in designs bent of spinal column and cartilege, spun in the sack, and a piece of tin in cardboard tagged around the twist to keep the sack closed. It is a heavy weight. But we tell ourselves that he would have just thrown them in the garbage can otherwise. At least we can feed these creatures to other creatures, carnivores as the cycle goes.

Fifteen or twenty long pike, each one the signature of a pike, identical, cut from the same mold, and yet each one must have identity, its own dreams, its own birth-star; everyone is a specific pike, not just "Pike: 69¢ per lb." Each of them is *the* pike, the constellation of the "large, slender, voracious fresh-water fish of the genus *Esox*, having a long snout," is the point of an arrow, the pointed summit of a hill, the pick-ax blade (after which the fish itself, pulled from dark waters, was named). The basic fish, identity of the group, returns, like an Indian dancer doing multiple dances, throws off a thousand, a million fish in strict and proper costume as he crosses the geographical matrix with his feet in place: each of these fish is inhabited by his spirit, each takes life at the synapse of his prayer-chant; each dies back into the changing pulsing rhythms of the dance.

The pike are pulled from the sack, cut along a symmetrical line like a sewing stitch; the skeletal supports are pulled out; the flesh is stuffed with pancakes, potato skins, krumbles and special K and forced thru the axes and blades of the meat-grinder; this is fish-flavored, specifically pike-flavored cat-food; this is fish-flavored protein; this is damned depressing, interrupting one stately dance and turning it into mulch to feed the processes of another, destroying Blake's fish to feed Blake's anvilled cats. We do it at home; there is no package label with a picture of the original pike to restore the identity; this is bloody universal flow outside of language, homemade cat-food; this leaves the whole kitchen smelly and ambiguous, distorts all our pelts and carcasses, our foods. And this week at the U.N., chocolate chip cookies, made of fish flour, were offered to all the delegates; they did not even taste fishy. We are truly creatures of language; we are truly the smiths and carters of a kingdom of the sun.

Lungs, intestines, muscles containing the genetic memory of swimming strokes, of schools in shimmering step, stuffed into the meat grinder, supplying the precious metals, the iodines and salts, to the processed food. My hand closes around the soft and slightly warm body of the flesh; I am the butcher; I close my eyes to what I am doing poetically; "God, we can't live like this." I close my eyes, throwing up a blinding pattern, the edge of a beautiful sword used in unholy war, throw it up between me and the actions of my hands, between me and the temple I rip apart and undo. "God, we can't live like this," and yet we do live like this; I am doing what I have to do. I peel the skin, the protective scales, like disarming some ancient enemy; I unpeel my own skin, like taking a graft off one part of my body and putting over another, feeding the cats. I unpeel certain soft membranes and neurons, my own nervous system disoriented, blunted; it all comes out one grey mulch.

The cats wait around, mouths watering while the grinder turns. They are so anxious that they sit under a leak trying to catch the juices that spill, like mouths opening for rain. Fish after fish is returned to earth, like the wall-eyed pike, the Great Northern pike swimming downstream into the traps made by men, the perceptual traps in which men lock themselves, prisoners of the subjective processing of their bodies, like machines turning out, and putting letters of the alphabet on: Hershey chocolate bars, in Hershey, Pennsylvania. They swim thru water, thru their natural habitat into the great steel prongs of the grinder, an environment as hostile to such carbon-crystal flesh as great atmospheric Jupiter; they are turned out not as one fish ground into fifty tiny baby fish, as in cartoons, but into a grey mass, a nutritious mulch.

I think perhaps we will never be free until we stop eating animals. But this is impossible. I think perhaps we will never be free.

Takornâq, the Eskimo woman, describes how another of her race came to eat the flesh of her husband and children:

"At last the husband and all children were frozen to death; having no food, they could not endure the cold. Ataguvtâluk had been the strongest of them all, though she had no more to eat than the others; as long as the children were alive, they had most. She had tried at first to start off by herself, and get through to Iglulik, for she knew the way, but the snow came up to her waist, and she had no strength, she could not go on. She was too weak even to build a snow hut for herself, and the end of it was she turned back in her tracks and lay down beside her dead husband and the dead children; here at least there was shelter from the wind in the snow hut and there were still a few skins she could use for covering. She ate these skins to begin with. But at last there was no more left, and she was only waiting for death to come and release her. She seemed to grow more and more dull and careless of what happened; but one morning, waking up to sunshine and a fine clear day, she realized that the worst of the winter was over now, and it could not be long till the spring. Her snow hut was right on the road to Tununeq, the very road that all would take when going from Iglulik to trade there. The sun was so warm that for the first time she felt thawed a little, but the snow all about her was as deep and impassable as ever. Then suddenly it seemed as if the warm spring air about her had given her a great desire to go on living, and thus it was that she fell to eating of the dead bodies that lay beside her. It was painful, it was much worse than dying, and at first she threw up all she ate, but she kept on, once she had begun. It could not hurt the dead, she knew, for their souls were long since in the land of the dead. Thus she thought, and thus it came about that she became an inukto•majoq, an eater of human kind."

And so the kingdom of the sun was founded on earth, at the temperature of cold crystal and rivulet water. And so the warm sun loosens, moistens us; we think we are home; we relax our guard; we settle down; and eat; we relax in after-dinner togas and moccasins. Neil Diamond sings: "almost makes me think/those times can come again;" we are alive; we tingle; we build houses in these warm crosswinds, by these mingling rivers and fingers of commerce; we send our commerce out like children, seeds; we are camped in our longhouse on this beach of light; we are hard as crystal; light, rays in general, pass thru us and change us; we are monumental; we sing in the garden; the supper bell rings and the stars turn familiar with food.

And I thought I saw on the football field today, the Oakland Raiders vs. the New York Jets, the great animals of the forest engaged in keen competition for food, competition undulled by supermarkets and redistributive economy; the completed pass, the deer falls; the players build a fire and roast it; eat, break camp, and move on, downfield. Wolves, hyenas, monkeys, sharks, hornets; lions and tigers in wing formation; the microbes eating up precious seconds on the clock, these initial and hungriest of all beings. The Jets and Raiders stand on the great savanna of play, of honed competition, genetic knives, the great field of Darwinian survival, accident, and chance. Who can say at the beginning of the game which team is better? Who can speak of past records? As well as we know our history and our natural history, we do not see that certain events, otherwise equal, have different weights in the context of the play; a fumble wipes out a hundred thousand years of downfield motion. The seed ferns, the dinosaurs are driven from the field; their dynasty is undone, as the Caesars topple, or the New York Yankees are replaced by a strange and ugly creature arising in the Pleistocene. Events have hidden meanings; a single invisible ray, placed correctly, opens a whole universe of visible light; a single fish, bursting thru a bottleneck, opens an unknown galaxy to habitation and shape. Against the stars of ethnohistory the great genetic score is kept.

Celestial influence bears down; the pot boils; the positions of the stars are like burners: a superior force lies waiting above our heads. There will be no freedom until we stop eating these fish, and letting their bodies go bad in display cases, until we stop turning our perceptions into entropy, from which they reawaken like hibernating beasts and yellow

[99]

flowers in the spring. There will be no freedom until we stop cracking open the golden shells, the wheats and apples of the earth. For the metabolism of the earth is moving too quick, and the sun, though it appears to pour indefinitely of its dense molten body into the thin planetary sky, is unwinding like a ball of thread, and we must look to the stars for our feed; we must look to the seas, where the silver life chain begins.

The meaning of "The Day of Judgment" is that we shall all be here again, when it counts.

SECTION VI
A FEW MEDICINES

1

The gold water rises from the bottom of the bottle, from the cellular base of the dream. The ultraviolet light of the funeral parlor shines on the iodide paper; an ammonia gas arises from ammonia carbonate on two hot coils. The fumes cloud the window; water vapor condenses against the lens, in the atmosphere above the city, obscuring the picture, smog burning the eyes. The great mountains are buoyed up by flotation on the sea of atomic gold. The blocks sink in fluid until they displace enough mercury to equal their weights, equilibrium of giants, of super-races and super-teams. The cameraman runs along the surface, the camera shakes and the rich odors of uncertain images fly. The incomplete combustion of coal clouds the city, a sienna haze covering the buildings and decomposing the brick, even as the coal furnaces clouded Blake's London, the incomplete combustion of language and thought, leaving a sedimentary poetry, a marl, Dickens' *Bleak House* entering on spongy earth, and in marsh fog, the author in his damp room, converting the ink to script, paid installment by installment as he unweaves the fog of social relations and genetic origins, as he unweaves the fog of the industrial age, the fog of three hundred million years of stored fuels, or three billion years of planetary existence.

The cameraman runs around his bedroom, the trigger pulled; he shakes the camera at lamps, mirrors, bureaus, outdoor film absorbing the hidden red light of thought. The cameraman films thru the membranes, thru the focal points of genetic heat. The gold water rises, the coal burns. colored wood-chips are sown in the Christmas fire: malachite green, ferrous red. The pine tree sits in the living-room, gleaming at its nodes. Red cells replace the dying blood at the year's close, trains converging on the holy city. The gold water rises, the coal burns; the infra-red light of the Automotive Supply Store burns past winter midnight; the oxides and sulfates burn, the red light above the Torah, the orgonotic red light passing thru skin.

The chemist sits at his desk trying to complete the ring of life: six wolves, red-hot tongues, fangs, burning iron lodes in the north, each hot tongue biting on the tail of the wolf in front of it. Zosimos dreams the yellow water, boiling, sulphurous, divine; the copper man giving and the watery stone receiving. The bubbling kettle simmers over the flame; within, the boiling man, the acetylene, giving off its heat of formation, its food. The cannibals devour the cinnibar, and the dead man, who has undergone great violence, returns to life, revs up his motorcycle, and returns to the highway. The city burns, and a chemical is released, an imperfect octane, the molecules clattering, knocking in being undone, the air raid over the school house. The body is mangled, but a chemical is released, the vapor of dreams and cellular memories, bodily fluids and naked atoms from the crowns of suns, a film whose parts and images pass thru and into each other, and change and change each other, as softly as smoke.

The shellfish takes two bromine atoms from the nearby sea-water. The glands of *Murex brandaris* and *Purpura haemostoma* swell with purple, dyes for the royal robes, lacking the two bromines and found in the *Indigofera* plants of India and Mexico: aniline, from the Arabic *al-nil*, the blue substance, worth 60 pounds an ounce in the shellfish, now synthesized from toluene and acetic acid; no need to go to films if you can dream, isoprene units locked head in tail, head in tail, the same formula repeated like music, but each time a different oil: rose oil, lemon perfume, turpentine, eucalyptus oil, peppermint oil, Tyrian purple, all of them C_{10}-compounds, either hydrocarbons, or with oxygen blown thru them and the chains rearranged around the new partners.

So the alchemist sweats in his dream, seeking the unknown chain leading back to the stone: three dancing rings, farnesol of lime and zingiberene of ginger oil. The chemicals are isolated and his sleep grows deeper. Zosimos ascends the staircase step-by-step, ascends the chemical process, the elemental scale. He passes thru the guard cells of indigo, thru the stability of alcohol. He passes into the interior of the castle, and in each room there is a light burning, or natural light, and in each room something is happening, or has just happened. A dwarf is dancing and juggling, velvet red. A baby is born and the prince wears a plume, light blue. The king takes a girl from the streets into the royal blankets, quinine. The lead leaves a silver deposit on the bed-sheets, maltose. The dusty urn drips its ancient concentrated drink, calcium carbonate, limestone and dolomite white. Treasures and paintings are stored, bronze yellow. The queen conducts a dancing lesson, citral, lemon yellow. The king puts on his robes, *al-nil*. The cook returns to the kitchen, carotene and rosehips. The civet cat is brought into the castle on a pole, musky ketone. Wolves tear the maidens to pieces and dance with their white gloves in mouth, cadmium. The wolves return to the forest, cinnibar red. The dreamer sees himself in a mirror at the back of the room; an unknown woman in the mirror is rubbing his back, perhaps with alcohol, perhaps with egg whites, perhaps with her own waters; the color is transmitted light. Zosimos now passes from room to room in the castle, his moons in conjunction; the only separation is the cell wall, the equivalent of matter in the astral plane; each step lights a new light, a new level; on each step there is a room, an unnamed inhabitable planet.

Is process. Is the chemicals of the body falling apart into dream. The chemicals of dream falling back into the body. The gold blocks, bullion, stored in a fort, on a memory track: the philosophy of the Western World. And each figure Zosimos meets is dismembered into a more initial chemistry; the color code is broken; purple withdraws from wool; and the arms and legs of the king search for new combinations and compounds. The metals slide back along a tune, a squeaking bubbling sediment, which hardens in time, as the armor, the leather, the personality of the chemical. The vision flows into the bottle, thru a funnel, thru the ginger of a closed eye. The vision is stored in a bottle, memory spindles dyed purple and gold, not the nickel-iron core, but the electrical and cloudy atmosphere, a band taped to the astronauts' foreheads, a band they neither strain nor penetrate, nor does Zosimos; the band is the whole earth.

The dreamer seeks the solution to the metals; the dreamer seeks the solution to his history. The alchemist seeks the personalities behind chemical exchange. Origins begin in a dream, as in a Dickens novel; the dreamer awakes in the middle of on-going history; the future eludes him; he seeks meaning in the past. The dream is the city in the dark bottle, is the bottle in the dark city. The dream is the circle inscribed in the triangle itself inscribed in a circle, the zodiac marking clear boundaries to all our thoughts. We see thru it from moment to moment but never at any one moment. We are led thru the mingled senses as all one sense, but never separately down any of these gates. The dream is not vision; the dream is visceral deposit, chemical activity, carbon rings: links the senses of location and tonic to the sensual rose doors. There are more senses than five. There are even more than five senses of smell.

It is another, a waking dream from which we awake to an awareness of the brighter sun. We are the wet man; we receive; we are under an incredible crystalline weight. We see it sometimes, in a flash, three rabbits dancing on a brick wall. We can sense that we are made of it, gravitation thirty times that of the planets. We sniff it, and then the geese fly North-northeast out of divining range. We are made of chemicals, chemistry, are penetrable by chemicals, but, as chemists, cannot penetrate them. We lie on the surface tapestry of one visual dance, the pools of the Buddha, the two lions before the library. We feel but cannot see the loose energy beneath this surface; the chemist must feel, must make syntax equal to dream; in the penetration a form is precipitated, a symbol for chemical process, a pictograph of chemical process itself.

Virchow says that in one thousand autopsies he has yet to see the soul. But what is he looking for? Mass is energy in another form, a billion buzzing bees and solar systems forming an image on a photographic plate, an organic image in the womb. We are made of light, of motion. We are not steadfast machines, nor is any machine.

[105]

The wolves snap their circles in flame, disappear, reappear elsewhere. What does this have to do with chemistry? We cannot discern the chemicals but we *are* the chemicals. Kekulé presides over the autopsy, the puzzle of aromatic compounds; he works with substitution formulas; none of them succeed. "Let us learn to dream, gentlemen. . . . "

So his eyes drift from the chemical pad to the fire; the substitution ends; the gates open. What are we?

"I was sitting, writing at my text-book; but the work did not progress; my thoughts were elsewhere. I turned my chair to the fire and dozed."

There is no need to solve the numbers. They have their own solution, Kekulé dreams and Zosimos dreams, and it is the eternal dream of chemists, as even Mendeleev dreamed of musical notes in ascending order.

"Again the atoms were gambolling before my eyes. This time the smaller groups kept modestly in the background. My mental eye, rendered more acute by repeated visions of the kind, could now distinguish larger structures of manifold conformation: long rows, sometimes more closely fitted together; all twisting and twining in snake-like motion. But look! What was that? One of the snakes had seized hold of its own tail, and the form whirled mockingly before my eyes. As if by a flash of lightning I awoke; and this time also I spent the rest of the night in working out the consequences of the hypothesis."

The chemist dreams and the archetypal chemist awakes. The atoms throw out their unbound shells, and the chemical reaction binds them. The deck shuffles, and isomers pour out like magical interchangeable rings. The problem solves itself, passing from the magi of Atlantis, west to the Egyptian ring of eternity, North to the Platonic unity of matter, circulates in a sealed vessel of Hermes, dances within the fire, the cells of Kekulé's chemically trained thought, is the solution of the benzene ring.

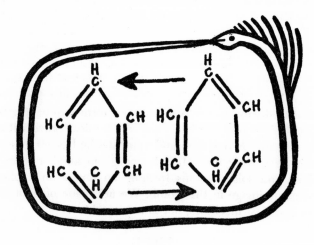

Who is to call the dream work a mere quilt of symbols? Who is to say that the archetypes are without lasting knowledge or that ouroboros is a convenience of notation? The benzene ring is a map of the temple, of Yesod, the genital realms of creation. Who is to say we cannot return East by sailing West? We are beings of light. We suffer from a chronic ailment, and it has gone on since the beginning and cannot be healed. We are only five minutes old living on a continent that doesn't exist, and even not existing moves a few inches a year into the sea. We dream, and in dreaming of fire, pass back into the bondage rings of light, organic lens of light. We cannot return to Shekinah, or the Garden, but in the dream of sperm passing, the chemical dream which is chemicals passing, in our own isotasy of chemicals, lit at the tips by proprioception, we can see an initial world of perfect rings, a world of which we are made.

This is a formal planet, a planet of eighths and octaves and binary nodes, measuring cup of the moon, measured as partial shadows and incomplete combustions, measured as the phases of the moon: phase by phase taking the metals out of their positions, mixing them; phase by phase inscribing the triangle, making the molds, deriving the ratios; a cake is baked; a car is set rolling on its wheels. In the dream Zosimos is approached by strange figures; these are the metals shaped as men, the metals prescribing a form that has nobility and speech, as both the planet and the metal choose Mercury to deliver their message, to analyze and divine their mute script.

So Chuck, for a short formal time, was able to set the boundaries of his daily, nightly dreaming (as a woman will mark out a plot for red tulips), set his boundaries by a mountain cabin, by the tarot cards which he put on all sides of him until they *were* his mountain cabin, by reading Basil Valentine until the stream poured alchemical waters and sun and moon shed on him their most alchemical rays. Astrology knocked at his door in the form of a woman, and he answered her; she was jealous of astronomy; so astronomy was driven from his bed; the stars closed in, and marked formal boundaries on all sides, rose and set within their fixed seasonal orbits, joined hands with the circle of cards and the ouroboros stream. And so Chuck became the master of the thing he taught himself, and even the birds were schooled in Basil Valentine, and spoke in signed patterns, an ornitholomancy. The mountain cabin was built of cards, and the limits imposed by the walls were the limits of meaning, the limits of intervals in the deck. The books opened themselves to the proper places, and everytime he pissed: a yellow flower, and everytime he shit, a yellow flower; he saw forty years into the botanical future without seeing anything. He saw a girl, whose only name was the color brown. Such were the formal properties of his experiment that he was taught in these things and learned the designations of their closed dance, and everything he touched, and everything we ever touch, is in these boundaries: earth, air, fire, water, the smoke rising from the great furnace of organic chemistry, exothermic heat, from the great carbon metabolisms of formal thought. Even the scale of the elements is periodic, not cumulative, and alchemy is a science of periods, music present in repetitions along a scale, isomers that sometimes take on the shape of metals, sometimes take on the shape of men.

He who makes gold will be gold. He who was tin, and pre-tin, is now hammered into carbon rings, and works on the metal with skilled earth-hands. This is the genetic order of the Medieval craftsmen, the clandestine unions of glass-blowers, of window-stainers and indigo, and Marco Polo, the encirclement of repeating cards and numbers, the training of apprentices, the bringing back of camels and elephants and Indians. The rings are closed but the manner of the rings is open. The chemicals are closed, but house after house appears at our fingertips, house after house, and sometimes we build them, and sometimes we live in them, and sometimes we are, in fact, the houses, the secretory snails.

2

Energy settles in muddy waters, silts, salts, drop by drop, trituration thru the clouds, a dim morning fog over the decanter, moss hanging from the trees, Crocodile rises simultaneous with mud, Seminoles retreating to the last genetic strands. The poisons are flesh, skin, life; the poisons are clouds, sunlight, winter glaze ice, hugging the telephone lines, the nervous system, bringing them down. The dream is of warfare in the swamp, biota and microbes, but all we hear is the steady drip, blood against stone, DNA into the hollow castle of ice.

The clouds mark the changing hormonal state of the planet, the releases of different glands at different times, slow maturation of streams, the elderly stream unable to hold its water and flooding the peneplain, losing its precious fluids to oxbows, clouds. Slow maturation of steams: natural gases and hot trapped waters that bleed when the bear is killed. Beneath the boat is mud, is shit, are the bodies of dead fish turning back into nitrogen, salt, releasing oxygen, fog, molecular odors, molecular colors turning, a rainbow of bioluminescence. Beneath the boat flow the medicines of the planet, flow Aconite and Belladona, flow Cadmium Salts, *Thuja*, and the rust of *Lycopodium*, the club moss: flow the very organic functions that cohere in man to a purpose, an organism; flow the loose interim organs of the planet.

"A patient comes with a pallid face, a rather sickly countenance, tired

and weary, subject to headache, disorders of the bladder and disturbances of digestion, and in spite of all your questioning you fail to get
anything that is peculiar. You prescribe *Sulphur, Lycopodium,* and a
good many other remedies in vain. But one day she says, 'Doctor, it
seems queer that my urine smells so strong, it smells like that of a horse.'
Now at once you know that is *Nitric Acid.*"

The poisons pour upon the continents; the poisons rise from the factories, from specific experiments, specific innoculations, radiation from
the sunless earths, the pathological earths singing and crumbling above
and within the uranium tune. The poisons pollute the bloodstream; the
astronauts whirl thru the circulation of the patient; his brown organs are
thick and rich, shitty, South America, Florida and the Keys, the West
Indies, the vex'd Bermoothes; clouds pour across his endocrine countenance; he is in a state of repose; at night his nervous system gleams with
new currents, sheds old cells and lights new lamps; he is trying to imagine
a position; he is deploying his cities in an attempt to call out his name.
He is alone, inscribed with Mercator's approximate design; he is all men
at once, all possibilities of men.

A single drop of moon triturates, a crystal in solution; gases are purified
at a molecular level, great winds, farts. The astronauts are pulled back in
their capsule, back to three weeks of medical examination in their sphere,
back thru the cloudy protective glands into the poisons that rate and
pace metabolism. They are medically hot; they have been burned by an
astrology that, for an instant, included even the powerful earth.

Chemicals resonate under the note she holds; the penis fills with blood;
the continental bladders discharge. The disease is what we catch from
you; it is the liquor you spill out in your urine, one part per million, smell
of your arm-pits, your perfumes. You are a cameo, a frog shitting in its
pants, chemical process of the digestive tracts. You leave what you are;
you are a giant and your germs spread in epidemics, plagues, the dirty
underpants of the drunk, germ warfare of the loveless, worms passed
from cat to kitten, passed in the genes: the disease incubating while the
child runs and plays, incubating while he is healed of the measles and
healed of the mumps, incubating because he can run only so fast, because
he is only second or third best, or because he is the star; the disease in-
cubates as what he is, a single unknown thing, and after a time he doesn't
recognize it anymore, obscured behind the more violent symptoms of
injury and virus; but the disease, though suppressed, lingers, and cuts
its way into each organ, slowly changing the partitives of life until life
itself is another thing.

Who can speak of the difference between healing chemically and
soothing psychologically when, drop by drop, the body is one continuous

chemical flask? Whatever we will become, including new states of mind, is carried in chemical code; the lightning of our thoughts passes over chemical lakes, excitation over a dormant solution in the Rocky Mountains, charged like the summer air: the planet is a single bath of linked chemicals, genes, joined by inlets and oceans, rivers, winds, and clouds; poison pass into solution, out of solution; crystals grow in DNA, the sacs of the sleeping water-snake. The doctor gives birth to his own specialized instruments, subglandular rubber pipes, suboceanic snakes; heals himself.

"The patients are so accustomed to their long sufferings, when the disease is chronic, that they pay little or no attention to the lesser symptoms which are often characteristic of the disease and decisive in regard to the choice of remedy . . . . Finally they leak out in some way and the patient says, 'I have always had it and did not suppose that it had anything to do with my disease.' "

The spray falls thru soft air tinting spring, spray on the lilacs, forsythia, spray on the robins and *Crataegus,* the hawthorn tree; the haws ripen in September, their juices webbed with the pus of dying stars. Spray falls like rain, endless sheaths of poison on the ball-field, on the players, cosmic radiation determining the averages, the gene pools; the newly-awaken robin flaps his weak wings in the dripping poison of day; even the eye is not perfect; even the visual field is sore and marred, the planet hanging in ambiguous space.

Spray falls on the cool hidden mints, on the catnip along the brick *Nepeta Cataria,* spray on the strawberry and violets in the spray-shadow of the yew. The helicopter passes over the hidden city, dividing its blocks by machinery. The windows are closed, cats sit on the sills looking up at the invisible sky; their owners, asleep in seepage of triturations thru moss, archetypal poisons and night sweat, turn thru the shallow film of noise on their brains.

The spray falls into the fresh dew; birds and squirrels sip the water. A woman dresses as a prostitute, goes among hippies to recover her daughter; the dwarves hide her in a cave. There is just so much; there is just so little. We can be poisoned so easily, one lick of the wrong juice and the day is ended, the nap in which blueberry jam on white bread is turned into poison, the mortal possibility of getting enough done. I will make. I am soft enough to be the sensing organs of a planet, and still I have enough shape to cull and collect the stars.

The doctor passes from house to house, diagnosing the diseases. He is following a ball of yarn that strings out of his back pocket. He cannot find the beginning. He interviews his subjects. He listens carefully to their descriptions of ailments, their choice of word, and he writes it down in phonetic script, whether she call it her "monthlies" or her

[110]

"show," whether there is a source to the pain, or merely a periodicity, whether the repetition is somatic or clearly literary. He goes to the homes to diagnose the women, to the factories to diagnose the men. But there is no antidote for the mines or for Pittsburgh steel. The mines *are* the disease; the men are the disease; there is no distinction.

In each house he hears the sound of water washing the dishes clean again, the lethal sound of river against stone, porcelain. His own feet drag thru muddy poisons, the counter-weight on his years. The clean water mixes with the liquid detergent bubbles, mixes with the spray; the water seeps thru the earth, to the base of the aquifer, drop by drop, the poison is the cure, is its own climatic justification, *Similia similibus curantur;* and now he sees the visible poison rise, soft against the indoor lights, and now he sees the things that have been going on so long they will not stop. He sits down at the kitchen table, under the lamp, and writes out the recipe. He prescribes the disease, ten more long years of it. What else could he do?

" 'I have been watching you, and you work like none of the many doctors I have met. I do not think that you can do a thing for me, but listen to my story. About six years ago I began to have crampy pains in my legs, sometimes twitching and burning and numbness. These pains were so bad that I could not sleep. For relief I'd get up out of bed, pound my legs, soak them in hot water, rub them with everything I heard of. I took a barrel of pills and gallons of liquids—no good. Finally I had a lumbar sympathectomy. That really was a mistake and I lost my sight for several weeks. The pain in my right big toe became so severe that I had it amputated. Now my leg pains are worse than ever. How is that for a case?' 'Not bad,' quoth I, 'you have given me a beautiful picture.' A picture of what? Well, the big five remedies of central nervous system disorders are *Agaricus, Phosphorus, Plumbum, Picric Acid* and *Zinc,* and this picture is that of *Plumbum.*"

The patient *is* his disease and will be cured by it. A new language with Indo-European words is taught; it is not Indo-European. It begins on a woody street in the hot summer of Mercury's first years. She is a young girl who rode a bicycle, a purse strung on the handle-bars; she stops by a stream to rest, her bike against the tree; tomboy, she grinds it out, pubic bone against pubic bone, the contents of the purse spread on the earth. Our cure is everywhere; our disease is a disease of the nervous system; we have it because we believe in the possibility of disease. We establish the doctors in their practices; we choose ours from their lists of symptoms; everything is possible. If we read Jung we have Jungian dreams: lightning breaking open stones, red molten cores turning into fire-places, the dog's flaming tongue. We believe in medicine, and we accomodate the

[111]

x-ray machine with stones. We buy the drugs as children that will be the diseases of adults. We are fed the diseases which, suppressed by ruddy health, burst thru the cherubic countenance under the erosion of anxiety, a ceaseless sea. But it doesn't matter; we are finally subject to disintegrating metabolism; we are finally subject to the running down of the astrological clock. Who cares what we call the disease and who we choose as our physician, our psychiatrist, our ears, nose, and throat man. It won't end though we suppress it. For as long as we live, it is ourselves.

Medicines congeal in clots, break and flow like glaciers under the rising Egyptian sun; our life is a constant crumbling of ice followed by a rheumatic re-freezing; for a time the antidote is a single part in a million of poison, agitating the organ, forcing it to be its own doctor, though on in years and retired from active practice. The organ, after all, has taken an oath to heal itself. A Center is formed for Advanced Studies, but there will never be any results; the stone breaks and flows; I am tumbling and dizzy; the hard forms are healed into a granular dream; the organs take over, making me my body, or my body me.

Now the warm shower on my neck, the shower curtain pulled, but the window liquid with cold muddy rain. A high wind blows the droplets; the moon adjusts the faucet so that hot and cold vary ever so slightly in tune. There is lightning in the sky, soft discharge as water, a break in the water, letting one circuit into another circuitry. Or it could have been a break in the wet cells of my brain: soft intermittent lightning, identifying with the brain charges the head with buzzes, wind pressing the glass to resonance, soft warm shower, oscillating currents of electric warmth. The glands on my neck are touched by planets singing like smooth tops; there is no difference now between the inward eye and the outward eye, between the indoor piped shower and the hot metabolic rain; I can see in or out, and the window, in any case, is a soft grey wall of cells. I am soft; I am yielding stone; I will continue to do what I have been doing: my cells are made of black-eyed susans and fifties rock and roll songs. My heart beats comfortably, the medical rain on my back fills the mouth with soup, pounds the neurons into their own inward submission, soft bloody rain running along the neck hairs, warming the continuous blood, root hairs, the parsnips sucking up triturations of sugar, cold sunny sugar from the pipes: growing in their herbal pots, in the garden of the homoeopathic physician.

Blood pours into blood, blood coming out of the pipes of the house; it is the house I live in, wake to, dream to. I do not know the difference, the water running on me, the thoughts thru me, the lightning on tired sleepy eyes, harmonics of hot and cold, scar tissue eased back into the original growth.

[112]

And madness itself, melancholy, hypochondria, is not felt as one afflicted organ, but passes thru every organ at the empathy, sympathy of its functions, permeates the body at the resonance of bone, the electrical resistance of any whole. The love is me, but the love is *for* you, as *I* am.

There is no disease: likewise, no medicine. The doctors look down upon the body in time like astronauts. It is a complete being, and they momentarily outside its history.

Physician, heal thyself!

3

Night falls; the stars call out their occult numbers, and occult numbers awaken on the earth. In the hospital a red baby is pulled from the forge, the alchemist's hands dripping with steel: the clock is set; the alarms are notched, and each one, like a glandular lake, will be sprung by a passing planet.

The ice melts; the heart beneath the land beats, each icicle releases water from above to below like a pulmonary; hence the upper cosmos seeps down into the lower, though the Northern Lights represent a chemical ascension passed only by the electricity of thought. Viral DNA pours down from the stars, lands in Okeanos, the cellular ocean of unscrambled cards. The evolution of viruses is simultaneous to the evolution of cells; the parasite duplicates the *materia* of its host, enters by the runway of identical matter; the virus is the host; the madman is the madness; they live in a separate universe ten times thicker and richer than this one; there is a conscious interphase of occult numbers to which we supply housing and location. Positrons, neutrinos hurtle into replicatory patterns, smashing mirrors, driving the king from his palace, entering from the sea, an alternate route to the North, an Icelandic kingdom in embryo, a kingdom whose original gates have been frozen with rheumatic ice: now the sun shines and the gates fly open. The usurper is hidden in the adjacent cell, listens to the king's heart beat; the heir apparent germinates one cell away.

The king dies: *"après moi, le déluge;"* le déluge is life.

The blue flowers grow from a kingdom of utter blue, aniline. Cézanne dips into shellfish pigments, into *Indigofera,* tomato oils, egg yolk: life replicates life. The cells of milkweed stick and grow thick in a corona; the lilac buds burst in a circle; the extended arm of the royal family holds up its blue goblets, balance in the rain.

Forsythia is a yellow woman with a shallower pouch. The girl tries on a yellow bathrobe, now a blue one—now a yellow one. The sun rises,

[113]

setting off a million springs. The king's blood spreads on water, is spread on morning toast: Christ's blood, the fruit of grapes and haws, rose hips and blueberry drupes; in Christ's blood the dyes are manufactured, retaining their genetic memory there, Tyrian purple, Judge Logan's logan-raspberry, osage-orange yellow, latex streaming from the pores, a milky lymph. Here are the relics of the ancient body dripping from the higher sphere, the snails and shellfish, the wines and sugars of Christ's life. The name is the crucifixion of the maple tree, *Acer Saccharum*, its wound drained, the sugars bottled in miracle-vials, the spirit rushing out thru the leaves into the hidden chamber of the sun. Christ's flesh, then, is the domestic grains, the crude scarry flesh of amaranth in its magical bustles and pomps, dwindling to rye, wheat, maize, matzoh, piki-wafers, Arnold's white, and Pepperidge Farm whole wheat. Christ's flesh is the crumbling mushroom, sporous yeasts bursting to fill the chromosomal chambers of grain. Christ lies in the swamp, spewing poisons, Christ invades his own body with ergot. We live in a temple of occult numbers, and numerology opens the deck, the key to the flowering plants of the Northeast.

So the text says to recognize William Forsyth's yellow daughter by the long soft lobes that extend beyond her petal cup; she is xanthic; her colors are xanthin; her relatives are the yellow crab and the yellow-throat warbler. Lilac is cyanic, cyan blood; his relatives are the blue crab and blue-jay; he is recognized by his long goblet with short drinking lobes. Both lilac and forsythia have opposite leaf nodes, two stamens: both are ruled by derivatives of the occult number four.

The key takes milkweed and sandvine out immediately, their sticky male and female joints have fused into a wet crown; they are keyed out with orchids and other flowers whose organs and genital shapes are twined: "stamens and stigma greatly modified from the normal structure and scarcely recognizable as such, attached to each other and forming a special structure in or near the center of the flower." The key pursues *Glecoma* (the blue ground-ivy) by its sailboat shape, the upper petal "gradually distended distally," the great lower lip reflected beneath the water. The green sailboats pass along the fence, their great pods broken in the wind and their beans strewn along the sea. The occult number five appears in the hawthorn, as in the heavens, "flowers perfect, regular, in compound or nearly simple cymes, or rarely solitary; petals 5, white, rarely pink; sepals 5, entire or glandular-serrate; stamens 5-25, arranged alternately in 1-5 rows; ovary inferior or free at the tip, the 1-5 carpels with as many persistent free styles; fruit a globose to ovoid or pyriform small pome, usually red or reddish, sometimes yellow, greenish, or blue-black, with 1-5 bony, usually 1-seeded nutlets."

[114]

The kingdom is hidden beneath a repetition of occult numbers, hard bony implements left by Azilian hunters, their twirled harpoons, their great needles with topological eyes. The kingdom is hidden by the megalith builders, the computers operating at the speed of sun-light, then as now: slave-labor of the algorithm. The lilacs weave around the lattice; the cat beds down in the flowers, yawns on the edge of the roof; the plane buzzes in the stratosphere, resonance of the bone; the pie is baked of haws and elderberries. Now the Puritan poets sail in beanstalks to an occult continent, land of the red man, Mercury, the fire in solution, *Rubus allegheniensis*, the common blackberry. The ice-cakes rumble; the clouds pour into the sea and viruses burn in the ionosphere, bright as weather. The great body's sensing apparatus begins to awaken, columns of polyps and blind cartilaginous fish; a rumble of occult numbers cracks the jelly; the planets begin to manufacture shape. What matter if the common man is but the archetypal image; the archetypal image itself begins with jellies scraped off the continental bone.

Forsythia grows over the garbage cans; the Detroit Tiger game comes from the radio in the next yard, the voice warmed to the resonance of hot tubes. The ice-cream man pulls out raspberries and vanilla beans; the substitute shortstop hits an unexpected home run. Planets hidden by the daylight sky sharpen, grind poisons in the mud, poison arrow eels shot into the enemy, marsh marigold medicines given by trituration, slow clock of the limestone cave.

The metals ring the earth at cymbal tune; the ear drums thunder. The haw hardens, congealed stone of blood, DNA an unbroken electrical circuit: berry, blood, roasted duck and venison. Not only are these in archetypal shapes, but chemically they manufacture the liquids of archetypal recognition and archetypal transfer, chemically they manufacture the disease piggyback the cure. Cymbals, drums, pound: this is *Os*, earth, the magical bone.

The meat is broiled; the bread toasts under the wireworm flame; nitrogen rises from the corpse, tobacco smoke filling the fields of the thirteen colonies. Honey; llama's milk cheese; beer; a candy nougat of cocoa, chocolate liquor, soybean, and peanuts; vaginal fluid: the world scrambles kinetically in the nose, air currents punning on objects that have no other resemblance. Wild cherries, cinnamon, vanilla, sherry, carbon atom linked by a single bond to a hydrogen atom, by two bonds to an oxygen atom, the carbon with one free bond on which to build the aromatic oils of aldehyde. A lily is not a mustard, but both manufacture the crude sulphur of the earth's body, hence onions and garlics are linked with the crucifers turnips and radishes. Bananas are found to bear a haunting resemblance to lavender and wintergreen: $C_4H_8O_2$, the pungent esters. The chemical chains cross all other forms of taxonomy and flood the consciousness with secret forms of resemblance, hidden affinities based on likeness of chemistry, likeness of magnetism. The food we eat is turned into us: but is it us even before we eat it? How can we prescribe medicines when the resemblance between objects is buried beneath chemical byproduct, the likeness of DNA obscured by variety of living forms?

Similia similibus curantur; age-old touchstone whereby the broken chains of pure medicine are healed again in individual patients, whereby the circuits of DNA are brought into their aboriginal circuitry. One resemblance after another underlies this thin veil of life; one resemblance after another, and on this basis the molecules replicate themselves, on this principle the ships pass from England to Roanoke, the liverwort completes its life cycle, the ribosomes setting sail with their message, potatoes and pumpkins and squash, the radish carried from China to the pre-Greek Mediterranean by migrating horticulturalists, comes to the New World by ship in the early 1500's: "For what Climate soever is subject to any particular Disease, in the same Place there grows a Cure—" (Robert Turner).

The occult numbers pour in from within; it is possible for patterns to wind thru sub-intervals of themselves, to break known symmetries and metrics with another order of numerology, giving birth to unexpected numbers. The human baby swims in the maternal ocean, its gills against the rich birth fluids; a similar embryo in the Atlantic womb generates in the distal proprioception of a starfish. The earth is born of number, thousands of teeming ratios, but these numbers lose their numerical character and become plants and animals which, in turn, are the designata for further numerology.

A film of the earth's processes is best made by playing with the circles on the movie camera as if they were planets, the speed wheel from Mercury to Pluto, the universes of foci on either side of focus, the F-stops from noon sun to twilight, the zoom from proximal to distal, the direction from positron to electron; the astrology must be slowed down and speeded up; the sun must go on and off; the focus must explore all the doors along the hallway, the structures leading to and away from the focused earth; objects must ride rhythmically on one another without regard for when and where they first appeared and were filmed; all this motion leads back to the chemistry, the film registering rhythms of protoplasm until the heart is beating in and out of focus, proximal-distal in great nervous sweeps, and the light varies as the cells of the perceptual field.

The great rush of sound onto the earth is silent, but there is another sound, lying behind the visual noise of the frog sexually croaking; it is the sound he makes by being, which begins a whole new series of octaves, the sound of his position, and the water-lilies growing, is the sound the radio-telescope, the stethoscope receives, is the wash of water onto the aural cavity, the hum of ocular and olfactory nerves, a crumbling of neutrons and the grey grey membranes of gas that pass between and within galaxies: these are the sounds of the visual field; these need no sound. Every other body is a black body, hidden by the distances of the speed of light. Only the stars, and our own sun, are bright.

The great rush of sound is silent, and the throb of sight is sound, is music, notes shifting thru notes, we can hear both ends of the band, of our history, at once, Ives says, "Old Black Joe" and the Yale Freshman song, a choir singing suspended in time, the cat clawing up the picket fence to pull down a butterfly, lies in the strawberries chewing it, white cat turns the universe on her nose in the catnip patch, jasmine drips thru evening tea, lithium thru salts of the brain; yellow forsythia turns into gold coins, commerce of the nervous system; polished trumpets blow; Mummery Drug is no more, and the orange cabs of Rexall's psychosomatic medicine take over; this event has a planet and a musical note; Ives mixes them; the needle jumps across his record; but Holst's astronomy is a deep gramophone rhythm cutting into electric grooves, an ancient and well-known march.

The chain is unbroken; the danger of life is in the food we eat. The Apache dance with their uncle, *Rana pipiens*, the Leopard Frog, progenitor of the Frog Clan. All human food is composed of archetypes, totems, is chosen from the texts of *materia medica*, the marshes and fields outside the factory-town. This is one unbroken current of DNA. The harpoon in the walrus shorts the system, and the woman is brought to trial before the shaman for eating food out of season; the bullet bursts the quail. We are damned eternally to the products of carbon, to the occult derivatives and derivations of our own flesh, affinities and affiliations, the occult number system for which our bodies (numerical also) are the designata again.

SECTION VII

E PLURIBUS

1

Nothing is visible except the field itself.

The crickets. The sun burns away fog.

The moisture and mist left in a spider web. Spider in the center, his threads to the end of it.

Everything is an event, a sign, a manifold.

The squirrel cracks the nut.

We are trying to get a fix on our time.

The distances, spooled pooled from the eyes. Everything is moist, to which add a tincture. Rose water from the petals which have sat four days in the iris. Sweet briar. White tartar. Horehound.

The rabbit sits in the distance. Sprung. The crickets.

The hippies who moved in across the street where old man time died one day (three ambulance calls in a week, then silence, and wild dandelions) are running over the lawn bareback on power mowers. It is an anomalous decan with which to begin the new year.

Tansy. Foxglove. Juniper berries. Rust of iron. Celandine.

It is by these powers that we are here.

Mass is energy. Flowers give off light when decomposed. Stars.

To my left, here on the porch, forest hides everything, so that the people in houses on the next street are broken into colors and fragments. This much I can tell: a buzz-saw cutting branches off the giant elm; the children collect them and cart them off. A German woman screams OFF WITH THEIR HEADS.

"Philosophers have at times thought to account for our vision by the image or reflection things form upon our retina. This was because they presupposed a second man behind the retinal image who had different eyes and a different retinal image responsible for seeing the first. But with this man within man the problem remains untouched, and we must still come to understand how a body becomes animate and how these blind organs end up bearing a perception." Merleau-Ponty.

The kids on bikes pass, cursing (hey, asshole), try out the brakes on the downhill. Lindy calls them proto-cars, not bikes at all. But trying to turn everything into, to imagine motors, modulated power under the torso.

It is never silent here. Even the beetles eat away mass.

"Whole Roses, Gilliflowers, Marigold, etc. . . . Dip half open flowers in a boiling sugar syrup and open the leaves carefully with a smooth bodkin: lay the flowers on paper in the Sun or warm room or oven." DELIGHTES FOR LADIES, 1602.

In any color whatsoever shape size hue ratio   LIGHT

The archetypal man drawn first in   Light

The astral body drawn first from
The crab
The torso

Light

The sun so bright every needle in the blue and green spruces is defined. The grape vine wound around a rotting elm, shading an old tin garbage can, bright with intrinsic turning into light. Reminds me of the grape-vines of Vinland. For we live in Vinland. But the sun here will never be as bright as on the Moon, pure silver spilled off the bodies who walked as men, prime-apes, or the first. The Star Card, fingerlets running thru the sense of the universe, the pure mercurial iodide of touch.

"Thus the origin of the doctrine of matter is the outcome of uncritical acceptance of space and time as external conditions for natural existence." Whitehead.

Some of the grapes are green, some of them purple; some of them are green with purple shading. The young mulberry has grown to the height of the porch, all of its leaves different like snowflakes, serial homology of organs. We will be leaving this house soon, but the sun continues to constitute, is what body is. House.

Grape vines extending in clinging in   as a snake.

Bees in the coordinates of their own sensorium. Unprogrammed in and out of, or their own rhythm. A program.

On the Sun two children play, male child and female child, male fern and female. The orders of the But nothing is visible except the field itself.

"What we find in space are the red of the rose and the smell of the jasmine and the noise of the cannon. . . . Thus space is not a relation between substances, but between attributes." Whitehead.

There is a new year coming, and these golf courses will be turned into fields of daisies and phlox and milkweed. So the girl child executes her dance. And there are just some things we cannot see: the pure silver sunlight (thru the blue flower), the leaf who weaves his web with green, the language of the bees. Nor can we ever see how much is left can we guess how many beans in the jar except one person by luck of the Irish.

And Hermes and Bruno spoke of the living web of nature, of natural properties. Not taxonomies. But astrals. So that bees are astrals and flowers are astrals. Swatting a wasp and closing out a total passage of total light. The Hermetic, or Blakean vis to live. A caterpillar creeping along the sensorium. The organic source of particle-ular light. Vis Medicatrix Naturae. Or Reich described three main motions for his djinn: wavy motions, pulsations, and a west-east movement of the atmosphere orgone envelopes.

The world crowds in, in all its dresses, densities, forms. The tree loses molecules, absorbs sunlight, creates sugars and cambium bark, green color, gives off oxygen, bark cracks and falls, squirrels' claws pull down, gives off electrons, receives from the next orbit. Is invisible suddenly. Is an oak.

Our eyes must change to go by the ocean, and see the different waves, as the same sea coming in.

Is the replacement of matter which lies beneath our dreams, beneath all their symbolism, and never changes it, but the matter is replaced, and there is a base to everything, separate of the keys in which it sing/singes, and we cannot deny that we are made of a different batter every morning, though the same person goes to collect his breakfast. And the uncertain daystar that burns the Earth, it too replaced from core to corona, from unconscious to persona, to as close to pure fuel as we come, but still staccato pounding of the Earth. Which Reich thought he could release from dead matter, denying the second law of thermodynamics, bions, energy transitional between non-living and living matter, blue (whose hands reach into the wine-producing districts of Germany, and pull red grapes out of the blue sea, white grapes), Reich in the bion-producing districts of Maine, soaking up (not clamming or lobstering or fishing), but pure life energy from the sand, as the ocean's childbed. Blue. Distinctly alive as a handful of burrowing crabs. Vis Medicatrix Naturae.

"The Roses and Sugar must be beat separately into a very fine powder and both sifted; to a pound of Sugar, an ounce of red Roses: They must be mixed together and then wet with as much Juice of Lemon, as will make into a stiff Paste. Set it on a slow Fire, in a Silver Porringer, and stir it well; and when 'tis scalding hot quite thro' take it off, and drop it on paper. Set them near the Fire the next day: they'll come off." COMPLEAT HOUSE-WIFE, 1728.

We ourselves may be attached to these forms, and not motion, but nostalgia for the leaves of early fall, the color of blue in the regional sky, the accumulating wind, must be tempered by a chemistry, that change and not staticity is basic, and even memory is the glyph of change, that the images themselves are made of new material, as the visible sun is, and the old man sun falls dead on the Earth to be born again (hence, alchemy). Our interest is chemical diffusion of daystar down onto planet, thru all the storms in between, electrical and atmospheric. Or we are projection, movie of sunlight, shown to all and everywhere, and at this distance, measure a light dance, mime, made of light, Osiran, beginning with Egypt, that sand alive even now, the pyramids returned to bionic blue, a light show intercepted by the body of the planet. Which we pretend to name History. Come in.

2

And the sun stares out of the wet sky, converting electronic food into cellular food. Yellow milk; soft, from the millionth sphere fuel.

Yellow is the color of unbounded magic, of all possible histories entering the bound history of a world. Water, pouring onto the Earth as a unit, pouring into history, and the Carolina farmlands. The white light threaded of the stars.

Water and light: white gold. Adam Smith, looking into America: "To prohibit a great people from making all that they can of every part of their own produce, or from employing their stock and industry in a way that they judge most advantageous to themselves, is a manifest violation of the most sacred rights of mankind."

The Apollo astronauts, launched from this realm of osmotic speed, enter the swift motions that are common to planets. These men seem not to be moving, but they are approaching the speed of memory, when all human process is somatic. If flung at the speed of light, memory too would disappear and they would hurl thru the pure sensorium, the Magician piling the rose petals onto their eyes, their fingers, cramming their noses and mouths with sense. As long as their biological field is maintained, their bodies do not enter the higher order of speed. But in the distance they look back and see the Earth as an organic being, placed in its natural habitat, processing the sun as a giant American factory in the fields, as they too sit in an American factory; operational, the raw material pouring in, the freight of the landscape; the Earth sits, America sits, in the ecology of electronics, opening its valves to meteors, swallowing them in the organs of friction, nasal passages filled with the rare upper gases, nostrils an electrical perimeter of light; digestion blue, with brown blood, white gases, vapors, and the winds and cyclones of dispersal. Here in this factory sparks fly, a nervous veil of atmosphere, fingers rushing to discharge, to receive light. Ecology does not cease at the atmosphere, or with the sun, but endlessly pours onto the Earth.

Already the cotton gin is in the fields, the first factory, with its power looms and mule spinners, is in operation at Lowell, Mass., Americans eat standing up at lunch counters, and the children of the *Monitor* are at sea and beneath the sea, gun-turrets whirling. The High Priestess sits in the rocket age, midway between the four-dimensional sunlight outbound and the inward traffic of the Egyptian commercial world.

Great ships lay the Transatlantic Cable, and men rush out of the water at Hearts Content, New Foundland, bearing the line like a backbone, which reaches back to Ireland, and Queen Victoria on one end, James Buchanan on the other. A column of thought touches the sensoria of two continents, and animals, already wise, crawl ashore. George Westinghouse lights the streets of Pittsburgh with natural gas, and between the turning wheels and the men piling coal into furnaces, the mighty steam.

The robe of the High Priestess flows out of the heavens into the garden of the Empress, and on it the cold blue manufacture of the stars, and on it Joseph Henry's electromagnetism, and in the garden, a 50,000-acre bonanza farm, men drawing the giant-wheeled engines of the sun to reap and thresh and bind. The gold of the telegraph keys, the Magician's hands in the upper spheres, sets off the gold panic of 1869 in the lower spheres, and Thomas Edison, working the keys, perceives that the news of the gold is worth more than gold itself. What words has Adam Smith, here in the Qabbalistic sphere, where the news of our existence rushes thru the alphabet trees long before we are able to come, and the only return is to nature, leaving no one rich? Why does he think we toil for this origin, this state?

High in the Appalachians the river runs against the outer cortex, the igneous rocks of the Emperor. Where the water carries petroleum, it carries salt, and the river is rich with potassium and life, iodine and shape. Numb itself, water empties into the pool of total sense, igniting, and those five leaks in the angel's pitcher are the five entranceways into the human sphere, thru a single man.

"Dr. Oppenheimer, on whom had rested a heavy burden, grew tenser as the last seconds ticked off. He scarcely breathed. He held onto a post to steady himself. For the last few seconds he stared directly ahead and then when the announcer shouted 'Now' and there came this tremendous burst of light followed shortly after by the deep growling roar of the explosion, his face relaxed into an expression of tremendous relief. Several of the observers back of the shelter to watch the lightning effects were knocked flat by the blast.

"The effects could well be called unprecedented, magnificent, beautiful, stupendous and terrifying. . . . The whole country was lighted by a searing light with an intensity many times that of the midday sun. It was golden, purple, violet, gray and blue. It lighted every peak, crevasse, and ridge of the nearby mountain range with a clarity and beauty that cannot be described. . . ." U.S. War Department.

And so, in taking our sacred rights from Adam Smith, we find that the Qabbala urges us, in making love, to complete the circuit, man looking thru woman, electricity thru magnetism, into the Face of God. Woman is the coiled spring of differentials in the electrician's bath; man appears in the chemical energy of his penis rising thru the thermocouple, the hands of Charley Wheatstone, and one hand is on fire, one on ice, now one last time thru the corkscrew curl that Joseph Henry, the brash American, has added to the body: into the electrical field of the brain of the

[125]

inventor, of the Earth itself. Now she hangs her veil, on it the pent quanta of nerves and atomic speeds, which were once the pre-Medieval fruits.

The ticklish jellyfish, the female lobster is afloat with burning seeds. And shrimp of both sexes. But she has won the female vote and ended Prohibition, and the great foreign trawlers fish the oceans like crazy, pulling up hundreds of thousands of fish in their nets, investing every last cent in derricks and tows, and the unlimited pouring of fish from the North, the pulsing IBM keys under her fingers as she types out the messages of her employer. But fish still eat fish, and we are fish and the man still lies in his bed, in the veins and electrical stress systems of the ocean, ripping open the veil of the pomegranates, bursting their red sensual fluid in his own container of blood, releasing not blood, but the sunlight which falls on the oceans, not chemicals but thought, a nation of factories and smokes and underground tunnels leading back to the origin, thru the ever-open spaces between two pillars, thru the glacial canvass of the representational artists of flesh, clear thru the circuitry, the gate, into the white white daylight sun.

3

And a year later I come back to add a final note . . . .

The body, as the Earth, a whole man, walks with a cane, has his own ecology.

We support in our bellies a billion microorganisms, and there are three doctors in the nation that specialize in the ecology of stomach acid (one patient had diarrhea for eleven years from a bad allopathic drug which scorched the belly lining of lactose). . . . Or the forty year diarrhea of loose soils, glacial rock flour, 25,000 years at least (of man?) ridden off into the sea. The Old South—the belly lining—gone, and the black man in the city. Concentration of sunless energy. Requiring transportation to feed. As the new generation finds out in a muddy field in Bethel, New York. The reason for the location of our major cities: San Francisco, St. Louis, Chicago, Detroit, Manhattan. 450,000 people in a cow pasture must be fed, need water. Most of the organic chemistry of the Earth is now tied up in people, not coal or oil. People: the castle of hydrogen, carbon, and oxygen. 450,000 in a field: will grow like plants from vibration alone? radiesthesia? Sauer: "If we appeal to the sun for our salvation, we must build our visionary factories in deserts, along mountain fronts, and in great tidal bays, which fail to coincide with present distributions of dense and advanced populations, and which introduce additional charges in transport of power and goods."

Which is to say there's no free energy—not between atoms, not between molecules, not between cities, not between men. There is a freight charge, a loss of energy between here and there, there and here, as the train dwindles into a distance known as time, into the last century of mechanical power.

The Oasis overgrazed. The grasses tight about the Mayas' neck, choking them. How do we use what we have? except to stay as close to home, to each other as possible. This is the meaning of Bethel. As say opposed to Lou Goldstein, the daytime master of ceremonies at Grossinger's twelve miles away, who has herded people from activity to activity from *dawn to yawn* as they say locally, for twenty years. From dance lesson to swimming pool to golf course to lake to a tour of the kitchen to buffet food on all the tables. Not *Howl,* but I think you know the rhythm I mean, the accumulus of (a certain) madness. The produce here is plentiful, is used as division, so that it takes a hostess or dame of singles to bring people together, to pull mind and body into a single vector, seat them at the same table, which is why people have come to the Catskills for half a century: the ease of transport from NYC, the food, the possibility of meeting new people, the whole idea of a funhouse, with entertainment at night, and this is where the politicians from the City go during the summer of election years to shake hands by the pool.

So Grossinger's as one giant oblivious to another giant, Bethel, although my brother Mike, who would have spent the summer in the City if the city hadn't come to him, found a back road and brought over loads of food, Grossinger's Rye Bread, cookies, leftovers of a giant kitchen, again a question of freight, distance, and relationships between masses of people. The flow of food which underlies all. The terrain, not the microbes, as Pasteur himself affirmed on his dying bed. "Bernard was right: the microbe is nothing, the *terrain* is everything." The Black Prairies of Texas worn away, the smooth Plains of Central Oklahoma. Iowa. Man holds down the carbon crystal's energy; the planet waits. The lines of food change, steady as turgor, water breaking the dehiscence and flowing the other way. For one day Bethel was one of the largest cities in New York, or rather Yasgur's pasture was. But Gulfport and Pass Christian destroyed by hurricane, the houses ripped apart, the streets flooded into nonrecognition. The lines of power are not permanent, but worn down inevitably, as the Poles. Grossinger's is replaced by Bethel, even as in Mike's mind. The issue is direct shipping costs: the charge for freight from the Moon to here being staggering—the moon voyage notwithstanding/we still have to live somewhere. Whatever it is, it's not—as some commentators say—the discovery of the New World again; it is clearly uninhabitable, the collection of genes and loci being what we are and where we can live (derived from where we *have* lived). There are two opposing issues: man as the spiritual adventurer who goes wherever he

[127]

can, wherever materials will take him, who will go anywhere for a reason (Apollo, Bethel, and I'm sure the first made the second possible), and man as a daily earthbound creature, who must make it at home, without drugs, without help, without constant sound and moon-messages in his ears—DOMESTIC, DOMICILE, HOME, or the matter of ecology, that bellyful of hungry mites. This is the insoluble knot between Carl Sauer and Teilhard de Chardin. And the rock festival, with its head in the noosphere and its feet in Yasgur's fertile mud, illustrates our present bind. You can't graze cows on the Moon. Yet history draws the Moon Card. Not even a flag will fly on the Moon. And the hippies can't colonize Bethel. It's a typical Catskill weekend. You need a ride home. Mike stays, but all around him the noosphere in which he lived for a second withdraws. And if we turn the Earth into the Moon, this is where we're going to have to live, in direct sunlight, in pure noosphere, as one geographer says: with the Earth flattened out like a pancake to receive maximum sunlight, one giant rock festival straight from the sun, where sound is the same as light, and cells privy or able to consciousness grow and swarm around a magnetic center. I can't say what the Aquarian Age will be like. But already we know that this century has perpetrated the last great medical fraud, separating mind from body, and destroying the inland fields and organs as though they were not connected, and further inland forever in a circle, each to each—which is life.

* * * *

Soil and slope vary, man is not a product, totally, of environment but mixes with land, indistinguishable from it as from soma: rills, gullies, boulders piled in a field, these are the works of glaciers and men. And the forces of the Earth are always in motion, the condition wavers, as decay, breakdown, growth, maturity, river, soil, lagoon of the ocean, rush hour in the city, the water rushes in, the rocks tumble in Brownian sunsplash, like loess in the air, out to sea, as the shells, the calcia roll in.

Is more like a work of Machiavelli than the White Panthers, needing a prince and stern laws, so that people charged by different planets with equally just values do not overrun each other. It is not enough to be right. Stay at home. You can't tell a double agent from a triple agent from a quadruple agent: wind, rain, snow, ice, hurricane, town demolished, pressure solved. You can't tell a revolutionary army singing revolutionary songs from a counter-revolutionary army singing the same songs; in fact, you can't tell the revolution from the counter-revolution, Marxist Russia from mercantilist America. Justice is not enough; the work is merely for us to finish; we did not begin it. There is something which makes all men, even adversaries, equally men of their time, duplicates in a mirror. That is why we cannot tell Humphrey from Nixon, and why the North Vietnamese send men to the American bargaining table in

Paris. That is why people like a Giants-Jet game in the Yale Bowl (on the same day as the Bethel rock festival), where you can tell the difference between two teams absolutely the same. This artificial difference more powerful than who's right/who's wrong in Vietnam. It's not that war and peace alone have become confused with each other, but everything.

Men do get well: this law precedes standardized medicine, and is as certain as the revolutions of Jupiter and Mars. But what about the Earth, what about the turning of so many of its compounds into other compounds? Will we awake in a chemistry different than our own? Will anyone be able to digest this stone? Will there be enough energy left to get from Grossinger's to Bethel, let alone the Moon?

The terrain is everything (even in the etheric and astral spheres) for men. The surface is crawling with microbes, but a light, that of the local church, shines within. A lighthouse, blind but giving light and sound, before the shore.

There is land which underlies this nation, the soils leached, the Mississippi and Ohio turned into yellow rivers, the forests ripped up and burned, sea otter and lobster killed, salmon poisoned in the Great Lakes, a world totally wasted and lost by the Virginia farmers, mad on tobacco, the complex hydrocarbons broken down, not into good pure shit but a poison so indestructible that no liver could purify it, no whale of a planet could swallow it except the giant mammal-fish of time, longer than we can wait, unless we know something we don't know. About the atom. And the way energy is attached to the flesh of mass, and mind to its bodily shell.

No synthesis, synthetics can rebuild the lost world, known again as Mu, as the original mythology of a total virginal Earth, wisdom scrawled on tablets and in the populated air, no paper factories to list a million land deeds in Hancock County, but gift of the phenomenal land in which man is mirror and protagonist, so the crawling lichens of Mars make up its conscious chemistry. Consciousness is always a mirror attached, as light, to the unknown substance of which it is made. There is no way out of nature, for even the city, totally run on synthetics, is part of the natural world, the landscape, is sun and air and stone, is terrain shaped by the same possible agents, one of them being man,, here leaving his own intricate moraine, as New York indicates something different than a field of *roches moutonées*. The whole scenario has a giant plug into nature, and ultimately, thru breakwater into sun. And what Sauer is saying is that if we run out of everything else we better plug into the sun, which for Chardin is the only way out of history into the essential man.

The doctors who kill germs are breeding new and more durable viruses, as man is one such irritant of the underlying continent, and we seek to escape the cause of this illness, building dams and draining marshes, seeding the eye of the hurricane, canals leading two immune streams to piss into each other, eliminating genetic loci. The disease, the condition of our history, is suppressed, returned again in old age, is a dead black bird torn to bits by the cats, left outside our window, that we restore to the terrain, crystal into crystal, to the chemistry of the belly, where the microorganisms which we carry all our life begin again. There is no way out of man, so we better stay at home and figure out what we are, nor can you make one man out of another man, nor can a man live in a landscape without changing the phenomenology of both. Stones are piled one atop the other, carried by glaciers, make a New England fence, a certain type of architecture, stone profile, use of wood, a certain type of color left by the sun, distance from all the local rivers wash out into the sea. We change as what we change changes, wear what wears us. The planet is no different than the organisms it creates; and they are no different than the planet on which they live. And the doctor who goes to heal with opposites cures not the language but the voice, and floods more distant fields with poisons, cosmetics—so we cover our ecological blunders with pink ice, and the decay hastens—surely an ice age will come to these Acadian forests.

But for now, the life, the day, the food, the sun, the late afternoon hot as my skin. The flowers that are left.

NOTES

Page 14: theory concerning scapulimancy from Omar Khayam Moore, *American Anthropologist*, LIX, 1957.

Page 21-22: from "Mental Portraits of Remedies Familiar and Unfamiliar," by Elizabeth Wright Hubbard, M.D.; *Journal of the American Institute of Homoeopathy*, Vol. 58, 1965.

Pages 22 et seq.: textbook ecology material from *Fundamentals of Ecology* by Eugene P. Odom.

Page 57: "The Snake" by Al Wilson.

Pages 82 et seq.: Diane Di Prima: *Revolutionary Letters*.

Page 94: Roy A. Rappaport, "Sanctity and Adaptation," *Io/7*, 1970.

Pages 95-96: Knud Rasmussen in *Report of the Fifth Thule Expedition*, 1921-24, Vol. VII, No. 1, *Intellectual Culture of the Igllulik Eskimos*.

Page 98: *Ibid.*

Page 99: "Sunday Sun" by Neil Diamond.

Page 106: John Read, *A Direct Entry to Organic Chemistry*.

Pages 108-109: Edward P. Tine, Sr., "Repertory of the Homoeopathic Materia Medica," *Journal of the American Institute of Homoeopathy*, Vol. 58, No. 1-2, Jan.-Feb., 1965.

Page 110: *Ibid.*

Page 111: W. A. Boyson, "Some Meetings of Individuals," *ibid.*

Page 114: Henry A. Gleason & Arthur Cronquist, *Manual of Vascular Plants of Northeastern United States and Adjacent Canada*.

*Printed April 1970 in Santa Barbara by
Noel Young for the Black Sparrow Press.
Design by Barbara Martin. This edition
is limited to 1000 copies in paper wrappers
& 200 copies handbound in boards by
Earle Gray numbered & signed by the
author.*

RICHARD GROSSINGER was born in New York in 1944 and grew up in the City. He went to Amherst College, majored in English there, and then to the University of Michigan where he did three years of graduate work in anthropology. He is presently doing research in Maine on economic and ecological relations in fishing and coastal communities.

He and his wife, Lindy Hough, have edited for six years a journal called *Io*, a publication whose concerns are myth, geography, and the common source material of poetry, natural history, and physical science. There have been annual issues on Alchemy, the Doctrine of Signatures, Ethnoastronomy, and Oecology.

They have a son, Robin, born in June, 1969.